The Gurugram School Murder

The Gurugram School Murder

Leena Dhankhar

JUGGERNAUT BOOKS
C-I-128, First Floor, Sangam Vihar, Near Holi Chowk,
New Delhi 110080, India

First published by Juggernaut Books 2024

Copyright © Leena Dhankhar 2024

10 9 8 7 6 5 4 3 2 1

P-ISBN: 9789353457327
E-ISBN: 9789353458102

The views and opinions expressed in this book are the author's own. The facts contained herein were reported to be true as on the date of publication by the author to the publishers of the book, and the publishers are not in any way liable for their accuracy or veracity.

All rights reserved. No part of this publication may be reproduced, transmitted, or stored in a retrieval system in any form or by any means without the written permission of the publisher.

Typeset in Adobe Caslon Pro by R. Ajith Kumar, Noida

Printed at Replika Press Pvt. Ltd.

*To Manmeet Kumar, my spiritual coach,
who taught me courage and continues to teach me the
value of black, white and beyond*

Contents

A Note on Names   ix

Prologue: Blood Tracks   1

1. The Phone Call   5
2. The First Arrest   17
3. The Post-Mortem   29
4. The Press Conference   39
5. The Cremation   59
6. The Handover   63
7. The CBI   71
8. The Evidence   83
9. The Confession   93
10. The Reports   105
11. A Family in Despair   121
12. 'Tareekh pe Tareekh'   129
13. Road to the Trial   141

Contents

14. Three Families — 147
15. The School — 161

Notes — 173
Acknowledgements — 195
Author's Note — 197
A Note on the Author — 203

A Note on Names

This is a true story. However, in accordance with a court order, the names of the victim, the victim's family, the accused, the accused's family, the school and all associated staff, and the board and trustees related to the school have all been changed.

Prologue

Blood Tracks

The morning of 8 September 2017 seemed like any other morning at a private school in Bhondsi, thirteen kilometres outside Gurugram. At approximately 8.02 a.m., the school gardener, Harjot, made his way towards the boys' bathroom on the ground floor. Just as he was about to enter the bathroom, a panic-stricken student rushed out and told Harjot that something seemed to have happened to a young student of the school inside the washroom. Harjot rushed to check on the child, and on seeing what he did, immediately sped away to get help.[1] The day's routine was interrupted by Harjot's frantic and desperate calls for help. A few seconds later when the first couple of teachers reached the corridor outside the bathroom, they were shocked to see a little boy, Prince Thakkar, lying in a pool of blood. It was evident that the boy had reached the corridor by dragging himself from one of the toilet cubicles of the bathroom. Tracks of blood marked his attempt to seek help. He must have collapsed upon reaching the corridor. Everyone was taken aback by this gory sight, most of them shocked into inaction. There was blood all over the crime scene – the corridor outside the washroom, the walls of the washroom and, upon further inspection, one of the toilet cubicles was found overwhelmingly smeared with blood. The cubicle door was splattered all over with blood.

That the washroom had been the site of a ghastly act was beyond doubt. These fears were confirmed when a knife with a rusted blade and wooden handle was discovered in the bloodstained Indian commode.[2]

The horrifying sight of the little boy covered in blood would have moved even the most stony-hearted person. Most of the school authorities were too stunned to react. They were shaken out of their stupor when one of them, the school coordinator, yelled, 'Pick him up, pick him up!' She looked at Harjot, indicating that he should pick up the child. But Harjot was too nervous and didn't move. He couldn't muster the courage to pick up the bleeding child even though he badly wanted to help him. The coordinator then helplessly turned towards Amit Kumar, a conductor of one of the school buses, standing near the water filter. 'Please help me pick up the child and carry him to the car. It would be the right thing to do.' Amit dutifully rushed towards the boy and carried him to a Wagon R car owned by the school that was parked near the entry gate of the building. The driver of the car, a school employee, was ready behind the steering wheel.[3] The car drove away with Prince, who was accompanied by the school nurse and a couple of other school staffers, leaving behind the crowd that had gathered at the spot in a frantic state. In the meantime, at approximately 8.10 a.m., the school receptionist informed Prince's father that his child had been severely injured.[4] The police were also informed of the incident by the school's receptionist some time later.

As soon as the car reached Safe Hands Hospital in Badshahpur, Prince, who was apparently still alive,[5] was hurriedly taken to the emergency ward. However, he didn't seem to respond to any of the interventions. When the doctors performed cardiopulmonary resuscitation (CPR) on Prince, they claimed to have felt a pulse. They went on to administer first aid and emergency medical aid to the child, but it wasn't enough. The doctors were of the opinion that Prince should be taken to Artemis Hospital immediately as their hospital wasn't equipped to handle such a severe case. The school coordinator, who had driven there in another vehicle, did not waste a single moment and did as she was instructed. She informed Prince's father that they were going to Artemis.

Already under tremendous pressure, the coordinator broke down when the doctors at Artemis Hospital declared that Prince had been brought dead. She pulled herself together, before informing the school authorities that Prince had succumbed to his injuries.

1
The Phone Call

It was October 2009. Bhaskar Thakkar was given the good news by his family doctor. He hugged his wife, Jaya Thakkar. 'The result is positive. You are expecting again!' cried Bhaskar excitedly.

They had a beautiful daughter. Now all they needed to complete their family was a son. Jaya held Bhaskar's hand, smiling, hopeful. There was no joy that compared to the joy of parenthood for her. Bhaskar and Jaya lived in a rented house in Maruti Kunj, with Bhaskar working for an export house called Orient Craft Limited. They had arrived in Gurugram from Bihar in 2001, just as the city was emerging as a finance and technology hub. Worried that Jaya spent all her days alone while he was at work, Bhaskar thought it might be better if she stayed with his parents in Jamshedpur in the final months of her pregnancy.

And so Jaya moved there, but the two of them would spend hours talking on the phone. Jaya told Bhaskar about how she saw the baby's body forming in her womb on her regular visits to the ultrasound clinic. On the day of her five-month ultrasound, she phoned Bhaskar and exclaimed, 'I can see the little head, the tiny hands and legs.'[1]

Like most expecting parents, Jaya and Bhaskar formed a bond with their unborn child which was growing stronger by the day. Jaya would feel the baby kick and her excited daughter would often touch her mother's stomach to feel her sibling twisting and turning. On 7 May 2010, at around 12.11 p.m., Jaya gave birth to Prince Thakkar in Jamshedpur.

As a baby, Prince never troubled his parents. He was always happy and satisfied with what he had. Bhaskar and Jaya remember every detail of Prince's first steps and how 'Ma' was the first word he said. They remember it all.

Prince was very close to his parents. He shared a special connection with his mother, always clinging to her before falling asleep, his tiny fingers holding on to her hand. 'He insisted on sleeping next to me,' recalls Jaya.

'Whenever I was unwell, he would run to me

repeatedly . . . a few days before this incident, I was lying on my bed and the moment he saw me, he was worried. He asked me if he could massage my head and legs to make me feel better. And with a tinge of innocence, he asked me if he would be allowed to have a chocolate or an ice cream later on.'

In 2013, the Thakkars had moved to Shyam Kunj where they constructed their own house, an important moment for any Indian family. They lived in a gated community close to their children's school in Bhondsi.

Like many children his age, Prince loved sweet things and sometimes stole sweets from the fridge. Mangoes were his favourite fruit. Sometimes his parents would allow him to sit in just a pair of shorts on the cold hard floor and devour them. He would bite into the mangoes, the juices flowing everywhere, without worrying about getting messy.

Prince liked to cycle around the neighbourhood in the evenings. He did well at school and was even learning how to play the piano. Like many children, every time he heard an airplane in the distance, he would run to the roof of the house and look up at the sky. He told his father he wanted to become a pilot when he grew up.

Earlier in 2017, Prince had seen people roller

skating on television and begged his parents to buy him a pair of skates. A few days later, while shopping at a sports store in Gurugram, Prince even tried on a pair, and his mother was impressed by what a natural he was. But she was also scared he could hurt himself and so 'we promised him we'd buy the skates next year', Jaya recalled.

When Prince turned seven, Jaya and Bhaskar decided not to have any more children. They knew their family was complete. But this picture-perfect family was upended by a phone call on the morning of 8 September 2017. Life, as Bhaskar and Jaya knew it, would never be the same.

'Little did I know he would not live long enough to get his roller skates,' his mother would later say.

~

After dropping off his seven-year-old son and eleven-year-old daughter at their school at approximately 7.59 a.m., Bhaskar had driven back home. On the car ride to the school, Prince, who usually let his sister sit in front, had insisted on sitting up front next to his father. On reaching the school he waved Bhaskar goodbye and walked towards the building with his sister.[2]

The Phone Call

When Bhaskar got back home from the school run, he parked his car outside his house and rang the doorbell. Shortly thereafter, at around 8.10 a.m., the phone rang.[3] The voice on the other side, the school receptionist, was frantic. 'Mr. Thakkar, please rush to Safe Hands Hospital. Your ward has been injured and is bleeding profusely. Please hurry.'[4]

It was evident that something terrible had happened. Bhaskar started shaking; he hadn't even been told if it was his daughter or his son who had been injured. He called back on the same number, getting through to the caller only on the third try. 'Can you tell me if it's my daughter or my son who's injured?' asked Bhaskar in a panic.[5] He was told that it was his son who was being rushed to the hospital. The receptionist apparently didn't have any more information that she could give him. He called out to his wife, asking her to drop whatever she was doing and rush to the hospital with him. 'Prince is hurt,' he said. Jaya felt her stomach turn as she switched off the gas in the kitchen and ran to the car outside.

Numerous thoughts crossed their minds as the couple drove towards the hospital. Irritated with the traffic, Bhaskar was desperate to quickly reach the hospital. He was hurriedly trying to make his way through the chaos, when he got a call from the school coordinator asking him to come to Artemis Hospital instead.

Finally, they entered the premises of Artemis Hospital, located in Gurugram's sector 50. The pair rushed to the emergency ward of the hospital. Jaya waited at the reception as Bhaskar ran to meet the concerned doctor, who informed him that his son had been brought dead.

Bhaskar was taken into the room where Prince lay, lifeless. He was convinced that the doctors were wrong and that Prince would wake up at any moment. To Bhaskar, his son appeared to be sleeping peacefully. But when a lifeless Prince showed no signs of opening his eyes, Bhaskar broke down inconsolably.[6]

As per hospital reports, Prince was brought in unconscious and unresponsive, and his body was cold, pale and drenched in blood. There was no activity recorded on the cardiac monitor. He was declared to have been brought dead at 8.37 a.m.[7]

Mustering all the courage he could, Bhaskar walked back to Jaya. He was unsure of how to break the news to his wife. He held her tightly and looked her in the eye before telling her that their son was dead. Jaya collapsed when she heard this, even as

The Phone Call

Bhaskar tried to console her.[8] He made some calls to a few relatives and friends who rushed to be by their side. He asked one of his friends to take Jaya home, in spite of her vehement protests. By now several employees from Bhaskar's office had also collected outside the hospital.

The drive back home from the hospital was one that Jaya can barely recollect now. Her heart was sinking and her legs seemed to be giving way. 'My Prince cannot leave me. He can't leave me like this,' she cried weakly. By the time the car stopped outside their home, Jaya was inconsolable. She could hardly walk. Inside their living room, she wept until she finally fainted.[9]

Their neighbours who were at the house managed to revive Jaya. By then a huge crowd of family, friends, co-workers and neighbours had gathered at the house, inside and outside. Reporters from the print and electronic media had also rushed to the school, hospital and the Thakkars' residence to cover the story. The couple's daughter had been picked up from school and brought home. She learnt about the incident only when she returned home after her exam. Jaya embraced her daughter and let out a blood-curdling scream.[10] 'Be strong, Jaya, you have a daughter who needs you and you have to take care of her,' said a neighbour. His words seemed to have little effect on Jaya. Their daughter was terrified to see her mother in such a state.

The acting principal of the private school, and the school coordinator remained at Artemis Hospital until the body was sent for a post-mortem examination to the mortuary. The school nurse who was also there with them had left after the doctors informed Bhaskar that Prince had been brought dead.

On the directions of executives of the parent body that ran the school,[11] some of the school's staff members, including the coordinator, went to the Thakkar residence in Shyam Kunj later that day to offer their condolences. But the crowd gathered there, seething and simmering with anger against the school for Prince's murder, attacked them when they found out that they were from the school.[12] 'How could the school let this happen?' they asked. They were apparently abusive and even physically roughed up one of the teachers. Another one of the teachers apparently fell while rushing to avoid being attacked outside the Thakkar home.[13]

Inside, the Thakkars didn't even know that the teachers had come to meet them. Jaya would later say, 'Was it not simply inhuman of the school administration not to have made any attempt to stand by us during such a difficult time? All the teachers who claimed to love Prince were silent. It was all very strange.'

Strange it was. How does a child end up murdered inside the bathroom of a well-regarded and high-profile school?

2

The First Arrest

The school had informed the Bhondsi police station at 8.40 a.m. that a boy had been severely injured and was found in a pool of blood outside the bathroom.[1]

At 8.58 a.m. two policemen from the Bhondsi police station reached the school.[2] In the meantime, news of the violent and gruesome murder of a student of the school had spread like wildfire. At roughly the same time as the arrival of the first policemen, parents and media persons also started collecting outside the school. In a little while almost 200 parents had collected outside the premises. Soon they were barging into the campus, fuming. They were demanding explanations from the school authorities. But no member of the school administration had the courage to talk to the unruly mob of parents. The school was still functioning according to its usual timetable and examinations and regular classes were being held as scheduled.³ Soon the parents, desperate for answers, started smashing everything in sight: a glass door in the reception area of the 1265-student-strong school, a centre table, a landline phone, flower pots. Trophies and books came crashing down to the floor. Enraged at the murder and the perceived failure on the part of the school to protect a young child, and concerned, no doubt, about the safety of their own children, the parents went on a rampage.⁴ According to Neeraj Vashisht, a reporter from a Hindi news channel, 'There were rumours of people planning to set the school building on fire.'

The Gurugram Police had to intervene and stop the parents from causing any further damage. The police stationed themselves at the entrance of the school and locked the main gate to prevent more parents from entering the school premises. Outside, the parents and the press waited to get a hold of any detail pertaining to Prince's death. There were already scores of journalists and parents inside the school.

By this time groups of parents, journalists and staff members of the school had trampled all over the crime scene and contaminated it. The scene of the crime was utterly chaotic and had not been cordoned

The First Arrest

off. News channels were providing detailed 'live coverage' of the incident from the crime scene. The breaking news had created a stir in the city, leaving viewers stunned.

'Bring the camera closer . . . look at these bloodstains . . . capture them well,' instructed a reporter to his cameraman.

'This is the very bathroom where an innocent boy's throat was mercilessly slashed, leading to his death,' said another reporter on camera.

'This is the door the killer must have entered from, and this is the spot where he left the knife after slitting the child's throat,' said the reporter, pointing to the commode that had bloodstains all over it.

A few members of the media noticed a ventilator window without a glass pane inside a toilet cubicle and breathlessly started forming unsubstantiated theories about the killer and the window.

Parents, too, were trying to get a first-hand look at the crime scene. 'Excuse me, please,' said a parent as he tried to get past the crowd. But he couldn't bear the sight of the blood. He simply turned around and walked away.

Prince's black school bag – containing his school diary, five books, nine notebooks, a yellow plastic tiffin box with a sandwich, a yellow fruit box with pomegranate seeds and a steel spoon – and a blood-spattered water bottle were in fact picked up from the corridor outside the boys' bathroom by Anshul Garg, a student of class nine, and handed over to the school maid/cleaner.[5]

In an effort not to scare and panic the children in the school, the school authorities would even wipe away blood from the corridor, destroying valuable evidence.[6]

The first step the school and, more importantly, the police ought to have taken was to safeguard and cordon off the crime scene. 'Contamination' of crime scenes results in the destruction of evidence that could otherwise be used to solve a case. It can also result in evidence being discounted during a trial. But it was only at around 12.40 p.m. that the police properly sealed off the site of the crime and all the media personnel and parents were asked to leave the campus so that the investigation could be carried out smoothly.

By this time a number of key police teams had already come and gone. A forensic team led by Jyoti Rathi the crime expert from the Forensic Science Laboratory (FSL) team, had preliminarily examined

The First Arrest

the chaotic and contaminated crime scene at around 10.40 a.m. A dog squad had also searched the area and left.[7]

The investigating officer (IO) of the case, Inspector Narender Khatana (who took over from Sub-Inspector Shamsher Singh, the IO for the first two days) had reached the disorderly crime scene at around 11.11 a.m.,[8] after first going to Artemis Hospital. He ordered the school administration to hand over all the CCTV footage of the day.

The media trained a critical eye not just on the school but also on the Gurugram Police, who were under a tremendous amount of pressure to redeem themselves after the clear bungling of that morning. An unprecedented public fury had erupted.

∼

As the heat was starting to build up on the police, a blood-soaked and harrowed Amit Kumar, the conductor of the school bus who had helpfully carried the bloodied Prince to the car that took him to the hospital, had returned to the school. He naturally needed to wash up.

Amit walked over to the playground and washed

his bloodstained clothes with water.[9] He then joined the other bus drivers and conductors who were sitting in the playground discussing the details of the gruesome murder. Suddenly a constable walked up to Amit and said, 'Sir is asking for you.' Amit's bloody appearance had caught the eye of the cops who were desperate for a 'lead' in the case to assuage the baying media.

The constable led Amit to the PCR van where IO Khatana stood waiting for him. Khatana told Amit that he had a few questions for him regarding the incident.

'Come and sit inside the car,' Khatana ordered.

'But . . . sir . . .' Amit stood there, terrified.

'Get inside, we will interrogate you at the police station,' said Khatana.[10]

Amit knew he didn't really have a choice, so he got into the car, petrified. They drove off to the Crime Investigation Agency (CIA) office on Sohna Road in Gurugram. No one would know what had happened to Amit until later that evening.

The media and the parents would not know about

The First Arrest

this lead in the case until later. In the meantime, the police had to find a way to manage these increasingly restless groups. The police officials were finding it particularly challenging to deal with the inquisitive and aggressive media fraternity parked there since 9 a.m. They we clamouring for answers, both from the police and from the school.

In order to buy themselves some breathing space, the police phoned the school's acting principal and the coordinator, who were still at Artemis Hospital at that time, and asked them to face the press and answer their questions. Both the teachers reached the school by 2 p.m.[11] They went straight to the area near the reception where the media persons were standing with their cameras.

The public perception was that the school was to blame for Prince's death and also that the school authorities had been evasive. The school coordinator explained, 'Look, when the gardener found Prince and cried for help, I rushed to the spot and found the child lying in a pool of blood. We took him to the hospital immediately and informed his parents. I did what I could. We weren't sure about the murky details of this incident and thus could not comment on this issue for the longest time.'

Overcome with emotion, the school coordinator started sobbing and added, 'Why does everyone think we are being insensitive? We did all that we could to help Prince and his family. We also feel deeply upset about the loss of an innocent life. We took him to the hospital, which is the best we could do. We also feel the loss of the child ourselves.'

The school coordinator then walked away, refusing to answer any further questions.[12] The school's teachers were just the firefighters at the front line. Behind the scenes, the reputation of one of India's biggest education chains was at stake. Set up in the 1970s, the chain operates 186 schools where nearly 3,00,000 students pay close to Rs 5000 every month to receive 'good-quality English-medium education'. The group employs more than 18,000 faculty members. And there's big money involved too. According to one report, the group has a turnover of hundreds of crores a year, and is 'the most successful private school enterprise in the country'. The schools control vast tracts of land in some of India's most expensive cities.

The owners are a politically well-connected family. In 2015, the owners found themselves at the centre of a controversy for allegedly forcing teachers, staff and students to enrol as members of the Bharatiya Janata Party (BJP) by giving a missed call to a particular number. Apparently, teachers were set targets for enrolment and a part of their salary could be withheld if they didn't meet these targets. The school's parent group was no stranger to controversy then.

For the school, Prince's death was not just the loss of a beloved student but also a devastating administrative and PR disaster. It was another tragedy for the organization which hadn't yet recovered from the discovery of a six-year-old student's body in a water tank in its south Delhi campus in 2016.

3

The Post-Mortem

Doctor Deepak Mathur first heard about Prince's death a few hours after it happened. The whole of Delhi NCR was horrified by the details. But Mathur didn't dwell much on it. Having worked in the post-mortem unit of the Civil Hospital, a government hospital in old Gurugram, for over five years, he was used to death – and the process of examining cadavers closely.[1]

At around 1.30 p.m., a police van pulled up at the Civil Hospital mortuary along with an ambulance at its side. Inside the ambulance were Bhaskar Thakkar and his brother, escorting Prince's dead body. Bhaskar looked on, disoriented and disbelieving, as his son's body was handed over to mortuary officials for a post-mortem.

A few minutes later, Dr Mathur stepped into the

post-mortem room and saw the lifeless young boy on the stretcher, with two brutal cuts across his neck. His eyes were semi-closed. Prince's body had been brought to him for examination. Jaya Rathi, the FSL crime expert, was there too. This was the most gruesome death that Dr Mathur had ever encountered. Years on the job hadn't prepared him for this sight.

The body was kept in a deep freezer until the post-mortem could begin. The doctor knew that the media would be all over the hospital in no time, inquiring about the results of the post-mortem. He had to be extremely careful and precise.

Soon Sub-Inspector Shamsher Singh (the IO for the first two days) walked in with a file containing the papers that gave Dr Mathur the green signal to conduct the post-mortem.[2] At around 3 p.m. Dr Mathur set to work on the case that was now garnering national attention.[3]

Dr Mathur first observed that a strong force must have been applied to hold the child's head tightly before the fatal injury – the second of the two slashes to the throat – was inflicted on him.

One of the theories that the police was investigating was whether Prince had been sexually abused and then killed. However, Dr Mathur noticed that the child's

The Post-Mortem

clothes were intact. Prince was wearing a shirt and tie, a vest, underwear, shorts and a school belt. All of them were stained with blood. But his belt was buckled and neither the buttons nor the zip of his shorts were open. Only his feet were bare. His shoes and a single blood-soaked sock were found at the scene of the crime – they probably came off while he was dragging himself to the corridor. There were no signs of any struggle. After taking a couple of samples from Prince's clothes, Dr Mathur ruled out any sexual abuse.[4]

But outside the mortuary, the now debunked 'sexual abuse theory' was gaining ground. While Bhaskar was waiting outside, the gathered media persons mobbed him. He was asked about Prince's state of mind that morning. Bhaskar paused for a moment before answering, 'Prince was very excited as it was his best friend's birthday and he knew he would get chocolates. He loved sweets, you see.'

The journalist pressed on, asking, 'Do you think Prince showed any signs of mental or physical discomfort at night?' Bhaskar answered, 'No, in fact, he was eager to attend school the next day because of his friend's birthday.

The journalist probed, 'Do try and remember if he mentioned anything peculiar though.'

Once again Bhaskar paused before answering, 'Well, he was a little restless at night. I know he couldn't sleep properly. He said it was probably because of the power failure at night. But I know that we didn't have any electricity only for a short while.' The reporter then point-blank asked Bhaskar if Prince had ever mentioned any incident of sexual abuse or an attempt of the same.

Bhaskar dismissed the question. 'No, madam, never,' he said.

~

As per the mortality report of Artemis Hospital, where Prince was declared to have been brought dead, the child had a cut in the middle of his neck – this was the first of the two cuts that were inflicted on him – and a deep gash extending from his right ear to the left side of the neck below the mandible or the lower jawbone – this was the second of the two cuts to the victim's neck. This was corroborated by Dr Mathur. The post-mortem report identified the cause of death to be these wounds inflicted by a single-edged sharp weapon. Dr Mathur added that the weapon used for committing the crime was rusted. Both the food pipe and the windpipe were slit due to which Prince would have been unable to scream. He would have been able to produce only a feeble gurgling moan.[5]

'A considerable amount of pressure was used to make such a deep cut on Prince's neck,' added Dr Mathur. However, were it not for the second slash to his neck, Prince could possibly have survived. 'But the killer clearly overpowered him, thus inflicting the second, deeper wound which led to Prince's death.' Dr Mathur would later elaborate on how the first cut was superficial in nature; it wasn't very deep. It was the second cut that wiped away any chance of survival. All the soft tissues were damaged and the cut went right up to the child's scalp, he would later say.

The fact that the injured Prince had then crawled all the way to the corridor from the bathroom cubicle where his throat was slit twice was an action that would have been tough even for an adult, let alone a seven-year-old child.[6]

On being asked by the police about any possible bloodstains on the clothes of the murderer, the doctor clarified that if the assailant inflicted the injury on the victim from behind, the blood would either spurt forward or upward and not in the direction of the assailant. It could well be that the murderer had no stains on his clothes if he was behind Prince.[7]

The autopsy report was submitted at 5 p.m. It stated: 'The cause of death in this case is shock and haemorrhage following ante mortem single edged sharp weapon injury . . . its consequence were sufficient to cause death in normal course of nature.' The probable time between injury and death was just a few minutes according to the post-mortem report – though the doctors at the first hospital the victim was taken to claim he was alive and that they had felt his pulse.

After the submission of his report, Dr Mathur addressed the eager media about the findings. Bhaskar was in the audience. On being asked whether there could have been any chances of survival, Dr Mathur said it was next to impossible. Only an immediate surgery within two or three minutes of having sustained the injury could have helped Prince, he said, but even that would have been a long shot. After losing almost one and a half litres of blood, it was almost impossible for a small child to survive such a deadly attack.

When Dr Mathur was asked whether Prince would

have known he was about to die as he was crawling up to the corridor from the toilet cubicle, he said, 'While Prince was in extreme pain, I don't think he must have thought he was about to die. He probably just wanted to seek help. He was brave enough to crawl out of the toilet, but I don't think he had registered what had happened to him.'

4

The Press Conference

Outside the Civil Hospital, Bhaskar was desperate to know who had killed his son. He kept wondering why no one had been arrested yet. Why were there no leads? Why hadn't the school been held to account? The restiveness of the Gurugram school parents gathered outside the mortuary was also rising. The helpless father who had been waiting all this while to collect his son's body could not bear it any more.

He turned to his brother and said, 'Bhaiya, I will not collect Prince's body till the police catch the murderer. I want justice for my son.'[1]

His brother kept a hand on Bhaskar's shoulder and nodded. The family members and friends present with him outside the mortuary decided to approach the police commissioner and voice their concerns – they wanted the culprit nabbed immediately. The group started marching towards the busy roads of Sadar Bazaar, shouting slogans against the school and the Gurugram Police. They finally reached the police commissioner's office nearby. The crowd climbed up the stairs, shouting anti-police slogans, and occupied the floor outside the office, waiting to be heard.

The police were trying to comfort the agitated group.

'We are trying to nab the culprit. Please give us some time,' said a police officer.

'We want to meet the commissioner,' said a relative sternly.

The police's attempt to pacify the crowd did not help.

Deputy Commissioner of Police (DCP) Deepak Saharan approached the crowd with a sense of urgency.[2] 'Please give us some time. We are trying our best to crack this case,' he said, trying to calm the crowd.

Bhaskar stood up and said, 'I have lost my son, sir. Do you have any idea of my loss? Why haven't you taken any action till now?' Bhaskar broke down. 'What will I tell my wife? If my son had died in a road accident, I would have cursed my fate, but how can anyone explain such a heinous murder?'

The Press Conference

'I request you to give me some time after which I will get back to you,' said DCP Saharan to Bhaskar.[3]

'What do we make of such a grave incident occurring in a school? Does this mean that even schools aren't safe spaces anymore?' asked a concerned parent. The parents who had come out in support of the Thakkars were also fearful for the safety and well-being of their own children.

After a while, at 5.45 p.m., the crowd started dispersing. Bhaskar looked at his brother and broke down again. 'How am I going to face Jaya? What am I going to say to her?' he cried.[4]

Bhaskar pulled himself together and allowed himself to be driven home by one of his close friends. This was the first time since his son was born that Bhaskar would return home in the evening and his son would not be there.

The Thakkar residence was tense and miserable. Prince's cycle was kept near the main door, his cricket bat was placed in the corner of his room, his bed was empty and the sweets that he so loved lay untouched in the fridge.

That evening another family was missing a loved one. The forty-two-year-old bus conductor Amit Kumar had been taken to the police station by Khatana earlier that day. At around 5.30 p.m. Amit's twenty-nine- year-old wife, Mala, began wondering where her husband was. They lived in a sparse two-room house in the village of Ghamroj, a few kilometres from the heart of Gurugram. Amit had been working at the Gurugram school in neighbouring Bhondsi for the last eight months. He would leave home at 5 a.m. and be back by 5 p.m.

Nothing out of the ordinary had happened that day except that at around 4 p.m., as her two sons were playing in the mud-floor courtyard and she was cooking dal for dinner, someone had knocked on the door. 'I need Amit's identification papers,' she was told by a representative of the school standing at the door.[5] Mala did not think much of this request. People in India, especially the poor, constantly need to furnish papers in the ordinary course of their lives. She just assumed that the school needed them. 'Wait, let me get them,' she said. After showing the papers to the man at the door, Mala went back to her work.

When Amit still wasn't home by 5.45 p.m., Mala called him on his mobile phone but there was no

The Press Conference

response. She tried again, to no avail. When she tried the third time Amit's phone was unreachable.[6] She had no option but to wait it out.

At around 8 p.m. a group of people from the neighbourhood came to see Mala. They told her to put on the news. There, on the TV screen, was her husband of eleven years.[7]

The public relations officer of the Gurugram Police, Ravinder Kumar, had called for a press conference at the Sohna Road police station in order to announce an urgent update on the case. This was what Mala was watching on live TV in her home. In the presence of key print, electronic and online media personnel, the police announced that Amit Kumar, the school bus conductor, had been arrested for brutally murdering Prince. The police claimed to have examined the CCTV footage from the school earlier that day, leading to Amit Kumar's arrest. A little before the time of the murder, the police said, he was not only spotted outside the bathroom where Prince's throat was slashed but was also seen inside the bathroom by three boys who were changing into their taekwondo outfits shortly before the crime was committed. The fact that Amit Kumar's shirt was stained with blood and that he had subsequently attempted to wash his shirt made him a strong suspect in the eyes of the police.

The police had been under intense media scrutiny and at the receiving end of the parents' rage. The hope was that this breakthrough in the case would give them some breathing space.

Then in a made-for-TV moment, the police handed over the stage to Amit Kumar so that he could confess to the murder at the press conference itself. A slight man with a gaunt face and brooding eyes appeared in front of the press, limping. He wore a blank expression. He was surrounded by police officers on all sides and seemed to be having great difficulty walking. The press started asking questions, a lot of them to do with why Amit was struggling to walk. One of the police officers claimed that Amit was partially paralysed from before.

Amit then told the assembled media, in a staccato way, that he had gone to the bathroom on the ground floor of the school's red-and-white building to clean a knife he had taken out of the toolkit of the bus. Apparently, he wanted to take the knife home with him after cleaning it. 'I retrieved the toolbox from the bus and took out an old, rusted knife that had been lying dirty for a couple of days. I put the knife in my

The Press Conference

pocket and walked towards the main building. After urinating in the toilet, I felt like masturbating. While I was doing this, Prince entered the washroom. I pulled him towards me and tried to abuse him sexually. He attempted to raise an alarm and I was scared he would complain to the school administration about me, so in a fit of rage I pulled him into a cubicle and slashed his neck twice with my knife. Then I went out of the washroom. And minutes later, when the school coordinator asked me to help pick up Prince and carry him to the car, I agreed thinking no one would suspect me if I did this. I don't know what had come over me at that time. I did not want to kill him, but I feared he would create a lot of problems for me.'[8]

According to Bhaskar's lawyer Sushil Tekriwal, the police stepped in to try to stitch the story up better. They would claim that Amit 'got excited' on the morning of 8 September after touching students inappropriately while helping them get on to and off the school bus. The police would also claim that Amit had managed to unbutton Prince's shorts in the bathroom that morning and that the child started to shout and so Amit covered his mouth with his hand while he 'discharged' or climaxed. It was then that Amit killed Prince in order to avoid getting caught.

In the moment of Amit's confession, naturally a ripple of shock and revulsion coursed through the assembled persons. Viewers all over the country recoiled in disgust. Here was a man surrounded by policemen and cameras, confessing that he had cut open the throat of a seven-year-old boy in the school's bathroom after he had attempted to sodomize him. 'I was not in my senses,' said the conductor.

But something didn't seem right. The police wanted everyone to believe they had cracked the case in a matter of hours. After the initial shock subsided, a feeling of scepticism set in. Amit's confession felt rushed and staged. And, frankly, just unbelievable and far-fetched: a sudden urge to masturbate coupled with a sudden urge to sexually abuse a minor. Indeed, Amit Kumar appeared to be a puppet in the hands of the Gurugram Police, who seemed bloated with a sense of achievement.

Prince's family, too, couldn't believe the police's version of events. And, if anything, they would have been the most eager of all to get a sense of justice having been done.

'Now that the conductor has been caught, are you satisfied that justice has prevailed?' asked a reporter present in the house.

The Press Conference

Bhaskar seemed frustrated. 'I am finding this hard to swallow,' he said.

The post-mortem had clearly ruled out any kind of sexual abuse. Dr Mathur had pointed out how there were no signs of a scuffle and that Prince was still wearing his shorts and belt and underwear when he died. There were no signs of sodomy or attempted sodomy, as was being claimed. Jaya Rathi, the forensic expert, later revealed that she had even explicitly told the concerned police officials of this finding.

Other parents of the school were equally sceptical. The police were claiming that Prince had 'caught' Amit masturbating, which precipitated the sexual assault and then led to murder. But one parent, Saloni, wondered how Prince could have 'caught' Amit masturbating when a child so young would not have even known what Amit was doing. Rita, another parent, was sceptical of the police's story which implied that Amit by chance had the murder weapon on his person. 'Who carries a knife to the washroom? This is absurd.'

It seemed particularly cruel to accuse the person who had picked up Prince when everyone else refused and carried him to the car which would take him to the hospital. But this very fact, and the bloodstains on his shirt due to his act of kindness, were used against him by the police.

More troubling details would soon emerge that cast a shadow of doubt over the police's version. It was later alleged that Amit Kumar had been tortured while in police custody – that's why he was unable to walk properly.[9] The police's explanation that Amit was partially paralysed from before was denied vehemently by his wife Mala. 'How could he have been employed as a bus conductor had he been paralysed?' asked Mala helplessly.[10] Amit would later say, 'I was tortured, beaten, hung upside down and my head submerged in water by the police to get me to confess.'[11]

When a few days later, on 14 September 2017, Mala was finally allowed, after many unsuccessful attempts, to see Amit at Bhondsi's local jail, he told her he hadn't killed the boy. He said he had been framed and forced to confess. She believed him. 'How can this man who has never even scolded our children murder a boy?' she asked one reporter. Everyone in Amit Kumar's village believed him too. 'He is fond of children. He keeps to himself. He used to say that even looking at blood makes him vomit,' said a neighbour. Anju, another neighbour, who had known Amit for years, said, 'He is a simple man and can never commit

The Press Conference

such a crime. A man who can't even scold or hit his children cannot murder a child.' One of his relatives pleaded, 'Our Amit is extremely kind-hearted. He cannot kill anyone.' Even if they weren't loud and influential, a range of people came out in support of Amit – from Harjot the gardener to a school bus driver called Jairaj to sundry neighbours.

Those who met the conductor in jail saw that his hands were swollen and he was still limping badly.[12] These seemed to be signs of torture. He had heavy, sad eyes. Clearly life had dealt him an extremely raw hand. Gradually, a whole host of other evidence would be collated pointing towards the feebleness of the police's theory and their lack of diligence and rigour in the investigation. As witnessed by the children changing into their taekwondo gear, Amit Kumar had visited the bathroom at 7.54 a.m. – well before Prince had even entered the school building at 8 a.m.[13] In fact, an incorrect entry was made in the Bhondsi police station records that Prince entered the school earlier than he did, adding to the confusion.

Further, Amit Kumar didn't use the cubicle in which the murder was committed for urinating, according to these children.[14] He used a cubicle at the other end of the bathroom as that was the only one where the door latch was working. Indeed, Amit's fingerprints were retrieved on the day of the murder itself from this cubicle. But they were not found in the cubicle in which Prince's throat was slashed.[15]

Amit is said to have been at the water cooler near the bathroom around the time of the murder. This has been corroborated by a witness, the school bus driver Jairaj, who was also at the water cooler at that time. Harjot the gardener saw Amit chatting with Jairaj at the water cooler as he headed to the bathroom on the morning of 8 September, a few seconds before he would discover the injured Prince.

Questions were also raised on how Amit could have possibly walked around, squatted on an Indian-style commode and masturbated while keeping a nine-inch rusted knife – the murder weapon had a five-inch blade and a four-inch wooden handle – in his pocket, as the police claimed. Wouldn't the person carrying such a weapon surely get injured, especially while squatting over an Indian commode?

The police also claimed that Amit had previously been sacked from another school for 'sexually predatory behaviour' and 'misdemeanours'. But the school in question had never filed a case against him.[16] Nor was there any evidence that Amit had touched

The Press Conference

students inappropriately that morning or that he had ejaculated in the bathroom.

The more it was analysed, the more people realized that the police theory was full of holes.

∼

Jaya Thakkar was as puzzled by the police's version of events as Bhaskar. She wondered why and how Amit could have even noticed her son. 'My son never used to take the bus. We would drop him and pick him up from school.'[17]

But more than anything else, Jaya wanted answers from the school she had trusted her son with. 'If at all the conductor has killed him, why isn't the school taking any responsibility for the incident? Why should the school allow anyone to carry a knife to the toilet? Should the bus conductors and drivers use the washrooms used by children?'[18]

Indeed, rightly or wrongly, in the days to come these questions would keep surfacing in the media and in parents' minds. The parents were furious at the school and their rage was starting to boil over. The day after the murder the deputy commissioner (DC) of Gurugram district announced that the school would remain closed for the next ten days. 'We have to ensure that the investigation is not disturbed, which is why we have taken this step,' said the DC. This period would later be extended by four more days.

But that didn't stop the parents from gathering outside the school premises on 10 September in protest. The protests against the school spiralled out of control and resulted in the setting on fire of a liquor shop near the school.

The parents had many grouses and questions for the school administration – whether these had any realistic bearing on the crime being prevented was another matter. Why was school staff using the same toilet as the children? A government-appointed inquiry committee would later find that as many as forty staff members used the same toilets as the students.

Why was there no trusted female attendant to take smaller children to the bathroom?

Why was there a broken window with no grille in the bathroom?

Why did the school clean up the blood from the corridor instead of waiting for the police?

Why were people not screened for weapons before entering the school premises?

The Press Conference

And why was there no CCTV camera directly outside the bathroom? There were two cameras (CCTV cameras 5 and 6) in the vicinity but none outside the bathroom itself. Anurag Hooda, the public prosecutor for the case, would later say, 'Had there been camera surveillance in the corridor that monitored the entrance of the washroom, would anyone have dared to commit the crime?' Elaborating, he would say, 'Don't we all get conscious when we see CCTV cameras in lifts and public places? We do get a little conscious ... don't you think the absence of CCTV surveillance outside the washroom could have been an important reason for the identification of the crime spot?'

The case had created such a stir that union ministers Maneka Gandhi and Prakash Javadekar would call for an urgent meeting to discuss and plan a protocol to prevent sexual abuse and other crimes in schools. By 10 September 2017, the district administration and the CBSE would also set up their respective special investigation teams (SITs) to analyse the various norms that were violated in safety and security guidelines. There were even demands for withdrawing the affiliation of the school[19] – a move that would have, counterproductively, harmed the students and the parents even more.

The first head to roll was that of acting principal – she was suspended on 9 September. Roughly a week later, a new principal and vice principal would be appointed.

The spotlight was also shone on the functioning of the school's parent body. On 11 September, the northern zone head and group HR head of the school's parent group, were arrested.[20] They were booked under a section of the Juvenile Justice Act that deals with cruelty and crime against children who are in the accused's custody. The section carries a maximum ten-year jail term. The two were arrested specifically for 'loopholes' found in the security measures of the school, including a broken boundary wall, overlong grass which was apparently a 'snake threat' and the alleged presence of expired medicines in the school. It was a different matter that these allegations levelled by the Gurugram Police seemed to have absolutely no connection with the murder. One of the allegations, about the expired medicines, was later even found to be false. The men are now out on bail and in between court hearings.

Things were obviously fast spinning out of control and a special team was to go to Mumbai to interrogate the school's founders and their son, the CEO. On

The Press Conference

12 September, the wealthy and politically connected family applied to the Bombay High Court and obtained interim protection of a couple of days from being arrested. For the next few months the family would go from the Bombay High Court to the Punjab and Haryana High Court and to the Supreme Court to seek anticipatory bail. They were ultimately able to secure this.

5
The Cremation

The morning of 9 September, the day after Prince's death, Bhaskar opened the gate of his house and slowly walked towards his car. Accompanied by his family and friends, he went to collect Prince's body from the mortuary to perform the last rites.

During the fourteen-kilometre ride from Shyam Kunj to the mortuary, Bhaskar was filled with mixed feelings of dread, anguish and fury. It was past noon when the ambulance carrying Prince reached the Thakkars' Shyam Kunj residence. A grieving Jaya only got a brief glimpse of her son before his body was taken to the cremation ground. Jaya fainted from exhaustion and grief.[1] At the cremation ground hundreds of people had come to offer their condolences to the Thakkars. When it was time to light the funeral pyre, Bhaskar broke down. He wept while his younger brother Varun Thakkar, who had come from Jamshedpur, mustered the courage to perform the last rites. A minister from the Haryana government as well as a couple of MLAs were present at the cremation.

6
The Handover

While the Thakkars were rightly getting the support and sympathy of the establishment, Amit Kumar wasn't quite so lucky. On the day of Prince's cremation, as a judge announced a remand period for Amit, the representatives of the bar council of the Sohna and Gurugram courts took the decision of not providing any legal help to Amit, or to any other accused. This was a huge blow not just to Amit personally but to the very principles of justice and fair trial.

While Amit was in jail, his family was struggling to even find a lawyer. But a couple of days later, just when Mala had begun to lose all hope, a man knocked on her door.

It was Mohit Verma, an advocate from Rohtak. 'I can defend Amit in court,' he said. Convinced that Amit was innocent, Verma had come all the way to offer his services.[1] Mala was overjoyed, though she knew that the fight ahead would be far from easy.

Verma sat down with Mala to discuss the case with her. A few other people from the village also gathered around. As proof of their support for Amit, the villagers agreed to contribute towards Mohit Verma's fees. The session lasted for a few hours as they had detailed discussions about Amit's background and the intricacies of the case.

On 13 September 2017, Mohit Verma told the court that Amit Kumar was made to confess through torture and under the influence of drugs. Amit Kumar then formally retracted his statement.[2]

Mohit argued in court that Amit did not have any bloodstains on his clothes before he picked up Prince and carried him to the car. This was corroborated by the gardener Harjot, the school coordinator and the bus driver. He also added that the post-mortem report had ruled out any attempt of sexual abuse. So what was the foundation of the police's allegations?

Usually the family of the victim and the accused in a case are arrayed against one another. But in this case the Thakkars were also fighting in Amit's corner. Justice for their son also meant justice for Amit. They didn't believe the Gurugram Police's version of events

The Handover

and had mounted a desperate campaign to have the case handed over by the Gurugram Police to the Central Bureau of Investigation (CBI), the union's premier investigative agency. They simply didn't have faith in the police.

In fact, Bhaskar even brought this up with the governor of Haryana when the latter phoned him. According to Bhaskar, 'The governor, K.S. Solanki, expressed his condolence. When I requested him for a CBI probe, he told me that in case I wanted a CBI investigation before the preliminary investigation by the police, I could get that only through the court.'[3] Bhaskar and his lawyer Sushil Tekriwal already intended to approach the Supreme Court to force the Haryana government to hand over the case to the CBI. But when this became publicly known, all manner of pressure began to be exerted on Bhaskar, including in the form of dissuading phone calls from acquaintances of his. Bhaskar suspects these were made on behalf of certain police officials who didn't want the case transferred to the CBI at any cost. Perhaps an autopsy by the CBI of the police's performance and methods would reveal some uncomfortable lapses and errors?

On 11 September 2017, Bhaskar and Sushil Tekriwal entered the Supreme Court and made their case. At a press conference Tekriwal said, 'It appeared that the person caught (Amit Kumar) was not the real culprit. The culpability and criminality lay elsewhere.' The court of the chief justice of India agreed to hear the case, made several observations about children's safety across schools in the country and issued a notice to the Government of Haryana.

'After I had finished presenting my petition for the involvement of the CBI in front of the chief justice of India, I was told that the chief minister of Haryana, Manohar Lal Khattar, wanted to talk to me,' Bhaskar recalls.

'When I spoke to Manohar Lal Khattar, he categorically asked me why I wanted to go to the Supreme Court in the first place. I firmly replied that I wanted a CBI probe as I wasn't convinced with the role the Haryana Police had to play in investigating my son's murder.'[4]

By then the police's image had gone from bad to worse. On 10 September they had lathi-charged hundreds of anguished parents who had tried to enter the school premises in protest. They did this to disperse the crowd. The media wasn't spared either. The situation was spinning out of control and the optics for the police department of lathi-charging concerned parents and an inquisitive and critical press were terrible.

At around 3 p.m. on 15 September 2017, the chief minister of Haryana visited the Thakkar family. He was moved by Jaya's sorrow and tried to console her. He told her that he would help the police nab the criminal. But keeping in mind the growing unrest among the people and the scepticism regarding Amit Kumar's arrest, Khattar made an important decision. 'I am handing over this case to the CBI so that a detailed and thorough inquiry can be carried out. I will see to it that justice prevails,' he declared.

Bhaskar thanked him with tears in his eyes. Amit Kumar's family was also relieved because they believed the truth could now possibly prevail. This was also when the Gurugram and Sohna bar associations retracted their earlier retrograde resolution that no lawyers would represent Amit.

The chief minister also handed over the management of the school to the district commissioner for a period of three months.

The Gurugram Police were stunned into silence. Their reputation had taken a strong hit. They must have known that they had truly bungled up the investigation. And now the CBI would get the chance to look through their pipes to see what had gone wrong. More and more people were starting to wonder: was the police trying to protect someone?

∽

As it would happen, Amit Kumar would be granted bail on 21 November 2017. He was finally acquitted of all charges on 28 February 2018. The additional sessions judge of Gurugram said that Amit Kumar 'is hereby discharged ... as no evidence was found against him in the CBI investigation about his involvement in the murder of Prince'.[5]

7

The CBI

The CBI formally took over the Gurugram school case on 22 September 2017, and thus began an investigation that altered the course of the case entirely. The investigative agency appointed Ajay Kumar Bassi as the IO, handing over all documents to him. Bassi was thought to be one of the most honest and hard-working officers of the CBI.

On the morning of 23 September, when Bassi entered his office, his mind was busy with the details of the new case he had been assigned. In his eighteen years of service in the CBI, he had cracked cases of kidnapping and molestation of foreign tourists, the Telgi counterfeit stamp paper scam, cases involving explosives, narcotics, passport offences and so on. But this case was a category unto itself. It was one of the toughest cases he had ever dealt with.

He glanced at the file on his table. According to Bassi, the Gurugram Police had apparently tried to scuttle his appointment as the IO. Perhaps they were keen on someone else being given the job, someone who might go easy on the police who were suspected of having made grievous errors and miscalculations on the job.[1] But Bassi was determined to be fair and even-handed. He would relook at the case from the beginning.

As Bassi began going through the intricate details of the case, he realized that he needed to begin his investigation by relooking at the CCTV footage, questioning the witnesses that the CCTV footage revealed and also going back to the crime scene to regather forensic evidence. He was trying to work out the facts and view them from a perspective different from what was described in the existing police files prepared by the Gurugram Police. Essentially, he would start from scratch.

Bassi walked up to the LED screen in his room and turned it on. He started watching the CCTV footage which had been handed over to the CBI by the Gurugram Police the previous day. According to the CBI charge sheet, this is what the footage revealed:

The CBI

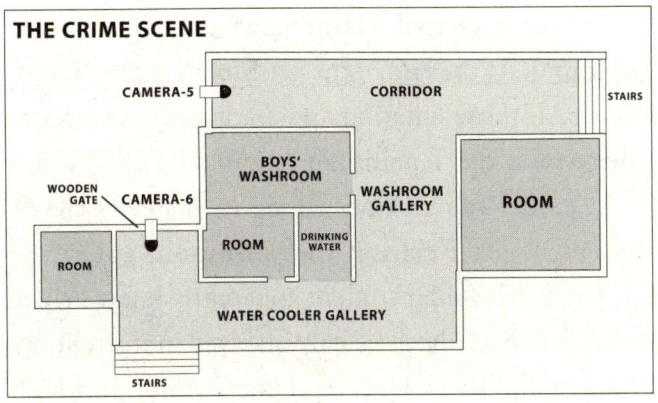

At 8.00.04 a.m. CCTV 6 captures Prince entering the school building through the 'wooden gate' used by the students.[2]

As you enter through the wooden gate, some steps ahead there is a flight of stairs going up to the first floor. Before the stairs there is a corridor on the left. It was known as the 'water cooler gallery' because the water cooler was in that corridor. If you have entered through the wooden gate the only two options are to either go up the stairs or to take a left on to the water cooler gallery. All those entering and exiting the wooden gate are captured by CCTV 6.

The water cooler gallery itself turns left on to another corridor called the 'washroom gallery', which has the entrance to the boys' bathroom where Prince was found. At the end of the washroom gallery is a 'T point'. All those entering and exiting the washroom gallery from the T point are captured by CCTV 5.

At 8.00.34 a.m. Prince, along with a class eleven student, is seen exiting the washroom gallery in CCTV 5.[3] The older student apparently knew Prince well as they were both heavily involved in the school's music group. There are several photographs in which both are seen performing together at a function.

At 8.01.03 a.m. Prince is captured re-entering the washroom gallery by CCTV 5. This was the last time Prince was seen alive before his throat was slit.[4]

At 8.01.23 a.m. the class eleven student seen earlier is captured re-entering the washroom gallery.[5]

At 8.01.58 a.m. Harjot the gardener is seen entering through the wooden gate and heading to the washroom. As Harjot is about to enter the washroom, the class eleven student comes out and tells him that there is an injured child inside, referring to Prince.[6]

At 8.02.35 a.m. Harjot exits the washroom gallery to get help for the injured Prince.[7]

The only other persons who were in these two galleries at the time of Prince's murder were Amit Kumar, the bus conductor, and Jairaj, a school bus driver. Amit was seen entering the water cooler gallery at 7.53.43 a.m. The CBI charge sheet would later claim that at 7.54.02 a.m. Amit went to the bathroom – that's when he was spotted there by the three children changing into their taekwondo gear. According to the charge sheet, at the time of Prince's murder he was outside the bathroom, at the water cooler, where he was chatting with Jairaj. This was confirmed by Jairaj.[8]

So who was this class eleven student? And what could he tell us about Prince's death? According to the CBI timeline, he was the last person seen with Prince. He was also the first person to have discovered Prince injured and alerted Harjot. Perhaps he could tell the authorities something valuable that would help them crack the case?

The student's name was Bholu. And even earlier on the morning of Prince's murder, before Prince had entered the school, the CCTV cameras had seen Bholu hanging about near the bathroom and the water cooler. He had repeatedly entered and exited the area that morning.[9]

Bholu's statements were recorded by the Gurugram Police on 15 September 2017 at his residence and again on 19 September 2017 by Inspector Narender

Khatana, the station house officer (SHO) of the Bhondsi police station.[10] These statements were recorded after the chief minister announced that the case was being taken away from the Gurugram Police and handed over to the CBI. Bholu had told the police that he had met his friend Tarun earlier that morning and that they had agreed to meet later near the water cooler, which is why he was in the area. While waiting for Tarun he thought he would briefly go to the music room to meet his favourite teacher. He did not find her there and returned to the area near the water cooler to wait for Tarun.[11]

Bholu further told the police that he entered the toilet on the ground floor when he heard vomiting-like sounds coming from there. When he entered, he saw an injured Prince in a pool of blood. He rushed out and told Harjot who happened to be walking towards the washroom that there was an injured child inside. He would also tell the physical education teacher when he ran into him on one of the upper floors that he had seen a child vomiting blood. Bholu was seen in CCTV 6, the one at the wooden gate, heading upstairs at 8.02.37 a.m., after Harjot had already raised an alarm.[12]

The CBI

When he gave his statement to the police, Bholu did not mention anything at all about Amit Kumar or having seen the conductor in the toilet where he had found Prince in an injured condition.[13]

Bassi reflected on the footage and on the statements given to the Gurugram Police till then. Fifteen schoolteachers were asked to look through the CCTV camera footage and identify the persons seen in the recordings.[14]

In his office, Bassi picked up the phone and made a few calls. Bholu and Tarun were called to the CBI office the next day, 24 September 2017.[15]

But before that, on 23 September, a twelve-member CBI forensic team arrived at the school to examine the crime scene.[16] The media was eagerly waiting outside the school for them to arrive. They had been waiting for almost two hours when the CBI team arrived in an Innova and a Tavera. As the guards opened the gates, one could hear the clicks of the cameras that had surrounded both the cars. A thorough forensic examination of the site was carried out.

On 24 September Tarun and his uncle and Bholu and his father duly arrived at the CBI office at the appointed time.[17] It is a time-honoured tactic to make persons about to be interviewed wait for some time. This could scare them and make them less resistant to authority, more forthcoming, less likely to lie. And so all of the interviewees were asked to wait. Bholu was made to wait alone inside an office cabin. During that time no one spoke to him. He could see people pass by but no one said a word. Bholu naturally seemed to be getting restless.[18]

Bassi finally called Bholu and Tarun into the room together. The two young boys walked in, introduced themselves and stood there, staring at Bassi.

'How can you call me like this, without any explanation?' Bholu allegedly asked Bassi.

'Don't try and tell me how to do my job,' replied Bassi sternly.[19]

In his statement to the Gurugram Police Bholu had mentioned that, on that terrible day, Tarun and he had met in the morning and that they planned to meet again at the water cooler – that's why he was hanging around that area. But Tarun denied this point-blank – either that they had met earlier that morning or that they had plans to meet near the water cooler. According to Bassi, Tarun seemed calm and confident while narrating his side of the story. 'Sir, I did not meet him that morning,' said Tarun matter-of-factly.[20]

According to the CBI, the CCTV footage would support Tarun's contention. Tarun entered the school building through the wooden gate at 7.54.24 a.m. along with his cousin Vikram and another friend. Tarun was then spotted by a CCTV camera on the second floor at 7.56.10 a.m. But Bholu would only enter the school building through the wooden gate at 7.58.04 a.m. and would stay on the ground floor throughout the time in question.[21]

This seemed to be an odd little inconsistency. So why had Bholu been hanging around the water cooler? And why did Tarun's and Bholu's stories not match?

8

The Evidence

Gradually, after the CBI took over the case, one thing started to become clear to them: Amit Kumar was indeed innocent. The Gurugram Police had been wrong to arrest him.

On 24 September, the CBI officials first interrogated Harjot and Amit Kumar separately and then made them face one another where they found that their statements matched perfectly. Amit recollected every move he had made on that fateful morning and it was confirmed by the CCTV footage. After this interrogation Amit was even made to visit the crime scene.[1] The CBI started considering the possibility that Amit might be innocent after all.

One of the main reasons for this was also Bholu's statement to the police. Prince was last seen alive entering the washroom gallery at 8.01.03 a.m. and

Bholu entered the washroom gallery at 8.01.23 a.m. According to the CBI, assuming that Prince took six seconds to reach the washroom where he was murdered, he would have been inside the washroom at 8.01.09 a.m. Assuming that Bholu also took six seconds or less to reach the area outside the washroom where, according to him, he heard vomiting-like noises prompting him to go into the washroom, he would have entered the washroom at 8.01.29 a.m., twenty seconds after Prince.[2] So, according to the CBI, Bholu would have entered the crime scene twenty seconds or less after the victim entered it. But Bholu said he didn't see Amit Kumar there.[3] Indeed, at that time, according to Jairaj the bus driver, Amit Kumar was at the water cooler with him.[4] When Harjot entered the wooden gate at 8.01.58 a.m., on his way to the bathroom he also saw Amit and Jairaj at the water cooler, before he saw Bholu coming out of the bathroom.[5] It would seem then that, given the CCTV timeline and the accounts of Bholu, Harjot and Jairaj, Amit was innocent after all.

The Evidence

While the CBI was satisfied with Amit Kumar's account of that morning, based on the charge sheet it is clear that they were concerned about some alleged red flags in the case of Bholu.

Not only did Bholu's and Tarun's versions of the story not match up but also, according to the CBI charge sheet, Tarun had levelled some serious allegations against Bholu. According to the CBI, on 15 September, after Bholu's statement had been recorded at his home by the Gurugram Police, Bholu phoned Tarun on the latter's cousin's number to ask Tarun to stick to the story he had just told the police.[6] But Tarun denied Bholu's version of the events to Bassi, and had earlier also denied them to the Gurugram Police – who did nothing with this information. This was yet another shocking dereliction on the part of the police.

The CBI thought it odd and suspicious that Bholu had been hanging around near the ground floor bathroom on the morning of 8 September. In the charge sheet they noted that Bholu was a class eleven student and his classes took place on the second floor. The senior students didn't typically use the ground floor bathroom. There was a bathroom on the second floor that Bholu could have used.[7] Indeed,

Bholu's movements seemed suspicious to the CBI also because, they noted, he had an examination that day, for which he was due to report at 8 a.m.[8] So the fact that he was hanging about the ground floor bathroom at that time was all the more weird in the CBI's eyes.

There were other elements of Bholu's story that the CBI didn't believe: there was the matter of Bholu saying he heard vomiting-like sounds coming out of the washroom, which prompted him to go inside to see what the matter was. But the CBI noted that Dr Deepak Mathur who had conducted the autopsy on Prince had declared that Prince would not have been able to make any sound other than a feeble gurgling moan.[9] In the eyes of the CBI this was yet another inconsistency. Prince would simply not have been able to make a loud vomiting sound according to Dr Mathur because of the nature of the wound and the filling up of his voice box with blood. According to Harjot, when he went into the bathroom Prince was lying in a toilet cubicle and was not making any sounds at all.

The CBI also managed to interview two students who were able to give some more insight into Bholu's movements that morning. They were the brother and sister Ankita and Ayushman, children of an army officer. Ankita, a student of class twelve, entered the school through the wooden gate at 8.02.10 a.m., twelve seconds after Harjot had entered the building through the same gate in order to go to the bathroom. As per the CBI charge sheet, Ankita said that when she was crossing the washroom entrance, she saw through the partially open door that Bholu was coming out – this would have been the moment right before Bholu told Harjot that Prince was injured inside the bathroom – with his school bag on his shoulder, wiping his hands with a handkerchief. This is another detail that didn't fit in with Bholu's statement to the police. Why would he have been wiping his hands?[10]

According to the CBI, Ankita's brother Ayushman, a student of class nine, entered the school through the wooden gate at about 08.02.28 a.m., eighteen seconds after his sister, and was making his way towards the washroom gallery. According to his statement, as he passed by Bholu, who was walking in the opposite direction, Bholu smiled and they casually shook hands. Ayushman felt that Bholu's hands were wet.[11] Again, this doesn't fit in with Bholu's statement where he never mentioned washing his hands to the police. Assuming Ayushman was right, why would Bholu's hands have been wet? As Ayushman approached the washroom, he saw a profusely bleeding Prince crawl out of the bathroom and try to take the support of a wall to stand up. He couldn't and he collapsed near the wall.

But perhaps the greatest red flag of all was that, according to the CBI forensic team which had studied the crime scene on 23 September, Bholu's fingerprints matched the fingerprints taken from the crime scene.[12] According to the charge sheet, 'The said fingerprint was lifted from inside the door near the lock in toilet no. 3 in which [Prince] was murdered.'[13]

~

On 28 September 2017, the CBI raided Bholu's house and seized some of his belongings, including his laptop, school bag, uniform, shoes, a mobile phone, a hard disk and several pen drives. According to the CBI, the search history on the mobile phone revealed that Bholu had allegedly visited sites that provided information on different types of poisons as well as how to smudge fingerprints. Bholu had allegedly also searched for ways to remove fingerprints from a knife.[14]

The Evidence

Where the Gurugram Police took merely a couple of hours to arrest Amit Kumar, after forty-six days of investigation, from 22 September 2017 to 7 November 2017, the CBI arrested the sixteen-year-old Bholu for Prince's murder. They definitively ruled out any attempted sexual abuse in the case.

9

The Confession

Bholu was arrested by the CBI at 11.30 p.m. on 7 November 2017. Earlier that evening he, along with his father, had been summoned by the CBI officials to their headquarters for the third consecutive day of questioning. He was arrested in the presence of his father and two independent witnesses, and the child welfare officers of the CBI and the Lodhi Colony police station.[1]

According to the CBI, before his arrest, in the presence of these witnesses, Bholu made a confession on camera. His confession statement was even signed by his father. But it must be noted that a confession given to the CBI or to the police has limited to nil evidentiary value in a court of law.

'I am not interested in studies, my interest is in playing piano and learning Western music. Since I am showing more interest in Western music, my parents were insisting upon me to concentrate on my studies. I used to bunk classes and go to the music room and spend time with my favourite music teacher (Western music). Since I am not attending classes and my performance in the school was below average, I was afraid of exams and Parent Teacher Meetings as my teachers may complain against me, so I was trying to evade the exams and PTM of the school. A few days before the incident I told my friends ... that I wanted to stop the PTM so I insisted to get me some poison for mixing it with the water to kill any child in the school so that the exams and PTM will be stopped. But no one brought me poison. The exam started from 06/09/2017 again which made me tensed. The first exam was English and it was an easy subject, I did that well. But the forthcoming exams were very tough and I didn't want to write them at all. So I decided that this time I should kill a child inside the school itself so that the exams will be stopped immediately. As a preparation, I purchased an iron knife from the local market ... [O]n 08/09/2017 ... I reached the school at about 08.00 a.m. My mind was restless as I was waiting for a chance to execute my plan of killing a child. Suddenly, I saw a small boy alone with a bag who was passing the washroom gallery slowly, I immediately thought that I can murder that boy. I did not know the name of the boy at that time but the boy was very small ... I asked him whether he would help me in taking some article from inside the washroom, the boy immediately accepted and I told him to wait inside the washroom and I followed him. I saw the boy standing in the middle of the washroom. I lured him towards the right side and took him to the extreme right toilet. When we entered the toilet, the small boy Prince (I later came to know his name) was facing towards the toilet and I was standing behind him. Immediately I took out the knife from the pocket of my pants and caught the head of Prince with my left hand and cut his throat with my right hand with the knife in an upwards movement. I did not have any blood stains on my hands as I assaulted him from his backside. I threw the knife in the toilet itself and rushed out immediately. As soon as I came out from the toilet I met Harjot Mali of our school and told him that one small boy is vomiting blood inside the toilet so please help him. I was very much tensed after this hence I started roaming in the second floor and first floor. Then at last I reached my exam hall Room No 10 in the second floor and I sat in my seat. After the exam was over I came to know that Prince had expired. I came home as usual and I came to know that the school was closed and exams were immediately stopped. I somehow got relaxed as I saw the news that the Gurugram Police had arrested Conductor Amit for the murder of Prince. I searched in the internet from my email id . . . how to remove finger prints from the crime scene. It was advised that we have to damage our own hand by charring or putting acid so I did not pursue it. Amit is not involved in this murder as it was I only who has murdered Prince.'[2]

There was complete silence in the room. This was a startling revelation, particularly Bholu's alleged motive for the crime. Indeed, to some it may even seem far-fetched that a class eleven student would kill someone just so that their examinations and parent–teacher meeting would be cancelled. This case was getting stranger by the minute.

Bholu was to be produced in front of the Juvenile Justice Board (JJB) on 8 November 2017, the day after his arrest. One could feel a slight chill in the air on the morning of 8 November. Outside broadcasting

The Confession

(OB) vans and reporters had stationed themselves in front of Vikas Sadan, the building where the JJB sits. Journalists were comparing notes on the murder case while waiting for the CBI officials to arrive with Bholu, accused of having killed Prince. Finally, at around 3 p.m., a white Tavera came into view and stopped at the entrance gate. The face of the accused had been covered with a piece of cloth and he was surrounded by policemen holding his hands. Reporters rushed to get a better glimpse of the boy.

The CBI officials and Bholu walked up the stairs of Vikas Sadan and into the courtroom. Sushil Tekriwal, who was representing the Thakkars, the public prosecutor and Sandeep Aneja, the lawyer defending Bholu, walked into the room. What followed was a lengthy hearing.

The atmosphere was tense. Bholu appeared in front of the judge, who started asking him about what had transpired on the day Prince died. Bholu was scared and nervous. He allegedly repeated the confession he had made to the CBI the previous day. According to Nisha Saini, an eyewitness, 'He also narrated the exact crime scene, how and why he murdered class two student Prince Thakkar.' Bholu wept inconsolably and fell to his knees, begging for forgiveness. He squeezed his hands, saying that he had not wanted to kill Prince and that he didn't know what had come over him. He apparently told the JJB that he had a younger brother himself and wondered what if someone had done this to him.[3] Nearly everyone in the room had teared up, shaken by this tale of a child being murdered and the young accused in the case. Bholu seemed to regret having committed the crime. He was offered water and asked to compose himself.

It is essential to note, however, that later that day Bholu's lawyer would tell the court that Bholu had been forced to confess by the CBI under torture, and that he was being framed for murder.

Earlier that day, at the hearing, the CBI had asked the JJB to give the agency custody of Bholu for six days so that they could carry on their investigations. According to the law, a 'juvenile in conflict with the law' cannot be put in jail or placed in a lock-up. Ordinarily, police remand of the juvenile is not granted either. But in this extraordinary case, the board agreed to give the CBI police custody of Bholu for a period of three days, not six. However, Bholu could only be questioned by the CBI between 10 a.m. and 6 p.m., in the presence of a member of the JJB.

The Confession

At all other times he was to be housed at Seva Kutir in Kingsway Camp, Delhi.[4]

Interestingly, Bholu himself was, at this point, reportedly willing to be handed over to the CBI. This is an especially interesting assertion when seen in light of Bholu's lawyer's submission later that day that Bholu's confession had been extracted out of him by the CBI through torture. On the face of it at least, Bholu seemed to have a cordial relationship with the officials of the CBI.

During the investigation, Bassi spent a lot of time with Bholu. One day Bassi offered to buy lunch for the boy.

'What will you have?' he asked.

'I want to have chhole bhature,' replied Bholu.

He was then taken to Evergreen restaurant in Green Park for lunch.

When Bholu asked for apples once, Bassi got him a kilogram of the best quality of apples available. Another time Bholu asked for chilli chicken for dinner, which he was promptly given.[5]

During the period of his remand, Bholu apparently cooperated with the investigation and he would even reportedly take the CBI officials to the shop from where he had allegedly purchased the murder weapon.

The shop was located in Anaj Mandi, Sohna, and the name of the shopkeeper was Pankaj.[6]

~

At the behest of Bhaskar Thakkar, on 15 November, his lawyer Sushil Tekriwal asked the court for Bholu to be tried as an adult and not as a juvenile.[7] According to a report in the *Indian Express*, 'The Juvenile Justice Act of 2000 was amended in 2015 with a provision allowing for Children in Conflict with Law (CCL) to be tried as adults under certain circumstances. The Act defines a child as someone who is under age 18. For a CCL, age on the date of the offence is the basis for determining whether he or she was a child or an adult. The amended Act distinguishes children in the age group 16–18 as a category which can be tried as adults if they are alleged to have committed a heinous offence – one that attracts a minimum punishment of seven years. The Act does not, however, make it mandatory for all children in this age group to be tried as adults.'

The report further states: 'As per Section 15 of the JJ Act, there are three criteria that the Juvenile Justice Board in the concerned district should consider while

The Confession

conducting a preliminary assessment to determine whether the child should be tried as an adult or under the juvenile justice system, which prescribes a maximum term of three years in a special home. The criteria are whether the child has the mental and physical capacity to commit such an offence; whether the child has the ability to understand its consequences; and the circumstances in which the offence was committed.'

Tekriwal told the court, 'The crime is chilling, horrific, monstrous and serious in nature and the accused, being less than eighteen years old but being more than sixteen years old (a juvenile in conflict with law) should be tried as an adult.'

The next step then would be to determine whether Bholu met these three criteria to be tried as an adult under the law. For this Devender Singh, the principal magistrate of the JJB, ordered Nisha Saini, the legal-cum-probation officer from the District Child Protection Unit, to conduct a social investigation and submit a report on the issue in fifteen days.

He also appointed Dr Joginder Singh Kairo, a senior clinical psychologist from PGIMS Rohtak to conduct a psychological assessment of Bholu.[8] These two reports would help the board determine whether Bholu was to be tried as an adult or as a juvenile. These reports would also shed valuable light on Bholu's backstory.

As the period of CBI custody was now over, on 11 November, after the JJB hearing, Bholu was sent to an observation home in Faridabad.[9] The well-built boy – according to some reports he used to go to the gym – was wearing a striped football jersey and trackpants, his face was covered with a black dupatta with thin white stripes and he was surrounded by CBI officials at all times. Bholu would stay in this observation home for juveniles till his eighteenth birthday in 2019.

10

The Reports

Although Nisha Saini had visited the observation home in Faridabad plenty of times, she was nervous about meeting Bholu. Nisha had driven to the observation home with a CBI team, including Bassi, on 13 November 2017. As she proceeded towards the main gate of the home, Bassi saw Bholu's uncle waiting outside the building. This was odd – 13 November was a Monday but family visits at the home were allowed only on Tuesdays and Fridays. So what was Bholu's uncle doing there? Nisha had already gone inside, so Bassi walked up to Bholu's uncle and inquired about his presence at the home on a day when relatives weren't allowed to meet Bholu. Bholu's uncle told Bassi that he was there because Bholu needed a fresh set of clothes urgently.[1]

When Nisha entered the building, she saw Bholu

talking to his father who is also a lawyer. According to Nisha, the moment Bholu's father saw her, he requested her not to tell anyone that she had seen him with Bholu.[2] Nisha nodded hesitantly. A news report the next day stated, 'Officials have asked for CCTV footage as meetings are not allowed on Mondays. Family meetings can only take place on Tuesdays and Fridays.'

Nisha met Bholu to interview him for the social investigation report she was supposed to write. It was then that he retracted the confessional statement he had allegedly given to the CBI and reportedly repeated in front of the JJB.[3] He claimed that he had not murdered Prince and that the CBI was framing him and had forced him to confess. Nisha recorded his revised statement. This was the first time that the accused himself, and not his lawyer, had said his confession was forced.

The new version that Bholu told Nisha was as follows: On the morning of 8 September, he had visited a temple to offer shradh prayers for his late grandmother. He got to school at only around 8 a.m. Thereafter he met a friend of his who asked him to wait for him near the water cooler. He waited there for about two minutes but since his friend had not shown up he decided to go to the music room to meet his favourite teacher, who had recently lost her father. The music room was locked so Bholu returned to the water cooler, but his friend was still not there. Bholu decided to go to the washroom where he heard the screams of a boy who was vomiting blood. He rushed out and told Harjot what he had seen. He would subsequently also tell a schoolteacher about the injured boy.[4]

This change in Bholu's statement left Nisha stunned.

Bholu and his father asserted that he had been beaten, hung upside down and had his head submerged in cold water till he had agreed to confess to the crime.

~

Nisha had a crucial role to play in preparing the social investigation report for this case. For this she had to meet Bholu himself and Bholu's neighbours, teachers, family and friends to find out what they thought about him.

One of the most touching experiences for Nisha was meeting Bholu's mother. Every parent loves their child unconditionally and she was no different. Both of Bholu's parents insisted that their son was a loving, considerate boy and wasn't capable of committing murder.

Nisha visited the school on 18 November 2017. She sat in a small room where she interacted with the schoolteachers one by one. Most teachers knew Bholu only as a boy who was often seen on stage playing the piano and his main interactions were limited to a few teachers.

Nisha submitted the social investigation report on 27 November under sealed cover to the JJB.

Dr Kairo, an experienced psychologist, submitted a two-page report as part of Bholu's psychological assessment under sealed cover to the JJB on 5 December. On 8 December the two reports would be opened in the JJB and shared with both sides, who were given time to go through them and use them to form their arguments. However, while the documents were shown to all parties inside the court, to maintain the confidentiality of the reports, they were not given to anyone to take outside the court.

The CBI's contention was along the lines of Bholu's purported, and now recanted, confession: that he desperately wanted the exams and PTA meetings

The Reports

cancelled as he was worried about his parents' reaction to his academic performance, that he had tried to procure a poison to add to the school water supply so that an incident could take place and the exams and PTA would be cancelled, that he was unable to procure such a poison and so he purchased a knife to kill a student to achieve his ends, that Prince happened to come his way on that dreadful day when Bholu was searching for a target, resulting in his murder.

So what precisely did the social investigation report and psychological evaluation say? These reports were only intended to help the JJB decide whether Bholu should be tried as an adult. But were they also in any way able to shed light on the CBI's claims?

According to the summary of the social investigation report, as quoted in the JJB order of 20 December 2017, Bholu had displayed certain behavioural issues in school. 'As per the statement of Ms Bhavika, music teacher of juvenile in conflict with law', his 'attitude' towards his classmates was 'aggressive' and he used to regularly shout at other children. He seemed to be frequently 'upset' and 'disclosed to his music teacher that his parents quarrelled regularly' which used to upset him.[5]

Bholu's favourite teacher mirrored this sentiment. According to the JJB order, she told Nisha that Bholu used to shout at other children in the school. He was 'very short-tempered' and 'restless' and lacked 'stability'.[6]

This image of a troubled child who took refuge in music was repeated often. According to Bholu's biology teacher Shamita, Bholu was a below average student but was 'good in music'.[7]

The school nurse, Manika Govind, would hint at a troubling history of behavioural problems and rule breaking. According to the JJB report, Manika Govind told Nisha that once Bholu had come to her complaining of vomiting. 'At that time he was under the influence of liquor.' The nurse could smell the alcohol on his breath. 'He also used a mobile in school' – which was against the school's rules.[8]

The order summed up the impressions of Bholu's schoolteachers as follows: 'Over all conclusion of Social Investigation report of juvenile in conflict with law shows that he is below average student in studies but good in music especially piano. He is aggressive in nature and also shouted over other students. He used to consume liquor and also used mobile phone in school premises. He is very short tempered, restless boy and also lacks stability . . . Juvenile also remain upset due to quarrel between his parents.'[9]

While the teachers at his school painted a picture of a troubled child, Bholu's neighbours had nothing but nice things to say about him to Nisha. According to the JJB order, they told her that Bholu was 'very peaceful and calm', that 'they never heard anything wrong about him'. He 'played with other children and also loved them'.[10]

The JJB order summed up the psychological evaluation as well. That report was prepared after Dr Kairo spent five hours with the juvenile at the observation home in Faridabad. Bholu was assessed on the basis of an intelligence test and an evaluation of logical ability and cognitive skills. The psychodiagnostic testing was conducted to ascertain, among other things, Bholu's emotional functioning and cognitive process. The JJB summed up the doctor's findings as follows: 'Dr Joginder Kairo . . . in his report conducted two tests . . . After both tests he gave his finding that IQ of juvenile in conflict with law is noted to be 95, in the category of average intellectual functioning.'[11]

The question before the JJB at this point was not whether Bholu was guilty or innocent of murder, but simply whether he should be tried as a juvenile or as an adult. In order to make this determination the JJB had to first see whether Bholu was over the age of sixteen. He was. Next, they had to see whether the crime he was alleged to have committed was heinous. The JJB concluded that it was. Thereafter the JJB had to determine, using Nisha's and Kairo's reports, whether Bholu had the mental and physical capacity to commit the offence in question; whether he had the ability to understand the consequences of the offence; and lastly, what the circumstances were in which the alleged offence was committed.

The public prosecutor started his argument saying that based on the social investigation report and the psychological report, the accused possessed adequate mental faculties to realize the enormity of the crime and the consequences that would follow such an act.

The law in its majesty tends to be merciful towards an accused who shows repentance for the act he or she may have committed. Even the prosecutor, in such instances, tends to soften on the accused. However, in this case, the prosecutor could not help but take into account the mental agony faced by the parents of the deceased. The prosecutor argued that not only was this a heinous murder of an innocent child, but

The Reports

also a complete breach of the trust that Prince – who knew Bholu from the school's music group and had performed with him at a school function previously – must have placed in Bholu as he accompanied him innocently to the washroom to help him out.

Bholu had initially allegedly confessed to the crime and begged the court for forgiveness. However, any sympathy that he may have garnered disappeared when he retracted his statement.

After careful consideration and hearing the arguments of all sides, the JJB on 20 December 2017 was to give its order. The crowd outside Vikas Sadan that day was buzzing. Reporters were present in huge numbers to cover the murder case. The parking slots were occupied by huge OB vans and the cameras were fully charged, ready to roll, not wanting to miss the minutest of details.

At noon the JJB judge and the legal counsels of both parties, Sushil Tekriwal and Sandeep Aneja, entered the courtroom on the first floor. The tension in the courtroom was palpable. There was so much at stake for both the parties.

The JJB concluded that Bholu ought to be tried as an adult. Notable in the JJB's reasoning was Bholu's alleged flip-flop regarding the purported confession he made to the CBI on 7 November 2017 and which he reportedly repeated to the JJB on 8 November 2017. The JJB concluded that the very act of distancing himself from his purported confession showed that Bholu had adequate mental capacity. 'This board can well recall the time when the juvenile in conflict with law . . . fairly explained the circumstances in which he committed the acts [that have] resulted in present inquiry along with the manner of commission thereof.' But now Bholu has 'narrated a different story excluding his role in the alleged incident' which indicates 'that juvenile in conflict with law also knows to cook up a story in order to save himself which in turn goes to show that he has adequate mental capacity'.[12]

Referring to Bholu alleging that the CBI had tortured him into confessing, the board recalled the personal hearing of 8 November 2017 when the question of handing Bholu over to CBI custody was to be decided. The board recalled that at that time Bholu had had no objection in being kept in CBI custody for three days in order to aid the investigation. The JJB remarked, 'It is not possible that CBI tortured him, beat him but despite that he requested to stay with CBI.'[13]

The Reports

With these damning observations, the JJB handed the case over to the district children's and women's sessions court, Gurugram, which would now take further the process of trying Bholu as an adult.

～

There was one point raised by the defence which would strike a deep chord with any rational person: if one were to take the CBI theory – that Bholu had committed murder in order to evade examinations and a PTA meeting – at face value, does this fact itself not show that the 'maturity level of juvenile in conflict with law is low'?[14]

Indeed, a considerable part of the CBI charge sheet that runs into several thousands of pages and that would be filed in court in February 2018 would focus on Bholu's bizarre motive to allegedly commit the crime. According to the CBI, Bholu had told Nitin, 'a close friend', that he was not interested in studies and 'never wanted to appear in exams and wanted to escape from [the] PTM ... Nitin also revealed that on the date of [the] incident, Bholu had first contacted him telephonically and then visited his house ... Nitin revealed that Bholu was happy that a student of his school was murdered and his exam and PTM were cancelled and he would get 10 to 15 days leave in his school.'[15]

As mentioned in Bholu's purported confession to the CBI, in the run-up to Prince's death, Bholu had allegedly asked several of his friends to help him secure some poison. According to Ayushman, a student of the school who knew Bholu from shared music lessons, in July 2017, 'when he came out from the music room and was wearing his shoes, at that time Bholu came to him and told him to bring poison or knife as he wanted to kill someone ... as he wanted to cancel Parent Teacher Meeting (PTM) as well as the exams'.[16] According to the CBI charge sheet, Bholu would similarly ask his friends to help him procure poison in August 2017. According to the charge sheet, these students told the CBI that 'Bholu was planning to mix up the poison in the water bottle of some child or in the water tank in order to kill some child or someone else with the motive to cancel PTM and postponement of exams'.[17]

The CBI charge sheet would assert that this incident wasn't the only time Bholu had allegedly made a desperate attempt to duck his exams and PTMs. 'Bholu had attempted to avoid the mock examination in February 2016 by complaining that someone had mixed some obnoxious substance in the water bottle because of which he was feeling drowsy. The documents collected from the Vidyalaya proves that he did not appear in the mock examination ... he was admitted in the hospital for about 3–4 days.'[18] Referring to the same incident, the charge sheet notes, '[His friend] also stated ... that when Bholu was studying in the 9th standard he brought poison to the school and he himself consumed [it] after mixing the same in his water bottle and put the blame on [someone else].'[19]

Clearly, according to the CBI charge sheet, Bholu was hopelessly afraid of exams and PTMs – even to the point of self-harm. According to the charge sheet, 'Ms Rekha ... Bholu's class teacher in Class 10th ... revealed that Bholu used to get annoyed very soon and never had permanent friends ... he was an average student ... his parents were worried about his education and his mother used to cry in most of the PTMs as her son Bholu was not good in studies.'[20]

Perhaps then the real question that ought to have been asked in the aftermath of Prince's murder was not why there were no female attendants in the bathrooms or why staff and students shared the same bathrooms or why the boundary wall of the school was broken. The real question was why a student as allegedly disturbed and vulnerable as Bholu, a student with a reported history of problematic behaviour, a student apparently driven to self-harm in the past did not receive the treatment and support he so desperately needed.

Even if Bholu did what the CBI alleged – and this is a matter that only a court of law can decide, and no court of law has ruled on this yet – is he not a victim himself in part?

11

A Family in Despair

Bholu's residence bears a deserted look today. His piano stands in a corner, dusty and unused.

Bholu's mother trusts her son implicitly and believes him to be blameless. She feels helpless when she is innocently asked difficult questions by her younger son whom Bholu adores. The little boy who had no role to play in this sordid drama often gets teased by other children for what his brother is alleged to have done. 'I am waiting for my son to come back,' says Bholu's mother. 'Only a mother knows the pain of seeing her children in misery.'

Both of Bholu's parents vociferously counter the claim that there was tension at their home due to their bickering. They dispute the fact that Bholu had any reason to be scared of PTMs, that he was under immense pressure to do better at school, that the pressure they put on him meant that Bholu was abnormally terrified of exams and PTMs.

His lawyer father said, 'There is no tension between my wife and me.' He further added, 'My child is good at academics. He loves music. He would never fight with anyone. The atmosphere at home is peaceful. We've never pressured him into performing better.'

Bholu's mother defended him saying, 'My son is neither aggressive nor misbehaved. He respected his elders and cared for animals. We always encouraged his love for music. We didn't force him to do better academically. He even learnt how to play the piano all by himself. That is the mark of an intelligent boy.[1]

'My son is multitalented, but has been completely misunderstood. I also feel that the teachers in his school never really submitted any written complaints against him. If my son was so problematic as the CBI has stated, wouldn't the school have taken any action? Or issued warnings?' This is indeed something that many people have been wondering.

Pulling herself together, she says, 'On the day of the murder, my son was in school all day long, and neither his uniform nor his shoes had bloodstains. How is it possible that my son's trousers did not even stain a little bit when the entire washroom was splashed with

A Family in Despair

blood? Moreover, a young boy who commits a murder does not have the mental wherewithal to spend an entire day at school.'[2]

Since the day Bholu was arrested his father has been running from pillar to post to somehow get his son out of this mess which could end up destroying his entire life.

'Given the way his neck was slit, there would have been a lot of blood spilling out. If the entire toilet was covered with blood, how did my son's trousers remain so clean? Also, the CBI claims that he purchased a knife. If so, why was it rusted? A new knife is never rusted,' says Bholu's father.[3]

He also asserted that the timing of the crime, according to the CCTV footage, does not coincide with what the CBI had stated in its case. (The CCTV timestamp was twenty-three minutes behind IST.)[4]

Reiterating his claim that Bholu had been tortured into confessing, his father explained exactly how the CBI was framing his son. 'They threatened him that they will shoot his brother if he does not admit to the crime.'[5]

In an effort to get their son back, the family is leaving no stone unturned. The father is now an active part of Bholu's legal team and acts as his advocate at some of the court hearings. He has also engaged some of the most renowned and expensive lawyers in India, including Sidharth Luthra and Tanveer Ahmed Mir, the lawyer who represented the Talwars in the Aarushi murder case. Tanveer is an expert at sowing reasonable doubt in the mind of the judge by focusing on an alternative theory than the one proposed by the prosecution. In this case there is one set of CCTV footage that led the Gurugram Police and the CBI to two separate theories. Both agencies had a different story to tell. This could be the weakness that the defence will exploit.

Ever since it became apparent and widely accepted that the police had framed Amit Kumar, there have been rumours that Bholu's father could have bribed the police in order to protect his son. He answers these charges without blinking, saying that his bank statements would have reflected such a transaction – but they don't.[6]

Bholu's mother refuses to believe her son could have killed a small boy. 'How can a boy who is so compassionate towards his younger brother murder a small, harmless boy?' She added, 'In fact, he told us that when he saw the boy vomiting blood, he was

A Family in Despair

immediately reminded of his younger brother whom he loves so dearly."[7]

Both the Thakkars and Bholu's family have suffered the total upending of their lives and the loss of their loved ones. Where Bholu's piano lies unused in his home, in the Thakkar home Prince's cupboard, his toys, drawings and bicycle have been left as they were on the day of his murder. Untouched, it seems they are still waiting for him.

12
'Tareekh pe Tareekh'

In the beginning, the media and citizens were morbidly fascinated by the gory details of the murder case. There was an insatiable appetite to know more and more. But the tragedy is that after the initial hoopla died down, and the studio lights were turned off, the fight for justice has been a lonely one for Prince's family. The case has inched its way through the legal system like any other case. The murder case is far from decided and this is a source of anxiety and frustration for both the victim's and the accused's families. The process is equally punishing for them both. And no one seems to care. Where earlier developments in the case used to be front page news, today the news of the case is tucked away in the city pages of one or two newspapers. Where earlier scores of parents would march for justice shoulder to shoulder with Prince's family, today everyone has moved on. But Prince's and Bholu's families simply can't.

There are more petitions and motions in this case, filed by all the interested parties, than can easily be kept track of. One major theme of the petitions has been the juvenile vs adult issue. Early on in 2018, Bholu's father filed an appeal in the sessions court challenging the 20 December 2017 JJB order that said Bholu should be tried as an adult. According to one report, 'The counsel for the 16-year-old accused had challenged the JJB order, saying it was "bad in law" and passed without giving him proper opportunity to present his case.' But in May the sessions court upheld the JJB order and confirmed that Bholu should be tried as an adult.

Bholu's father then went in appeal to the Punjab and Haryana High Court in July 2018. This time, however, the court would agree with Bholu's father and in October 2018 set aside the JJB order. The high court referred the case back to the JJB for reconsideration within a six-week period and termed the earlier process adopted by the board for trying the juvenile as an adult 'illegal'. The high court passed the order because of Bholu's legal team's submission that they were not given a copy of the social and psychological reports on the basis of which Bholu would be tried as an adult, and that they were not given a chance to challenge the reports. The JJB was to reconsider this basic question from scratch.

However, in October itself Bhaskar Thakkar filed a petition in the Supreme Court challenging the high court order. As a result of this petition the Supreme Court stayed the JJB proceedings and later scrapped it, finding loopholes in the order.

Over the next few years, the issue bounced around between the JJB, the high court and the Supreme Court as both Bholu's father and Prince's father filed petitions and counter petitions. In July 2022, the Supreme Court ruled that the accused must be examined afresh to ascertain whether he should be tried as an adult. In August, the JJB wrote to PGIMS, Rohtak, to form a board of doctors to conduct a psychological assessment of the accused, and in September, the accused was examined by a three-member board of PGIMS. In October, the JJB again ruled that the accused be tried as an adult as he had sufficient ability to understand the consequences of the offence and devise ways of escaping punishment.[1] In May 2023, the high court upheld the JJB's order, saying, 'The JJB has strictly adhered to all the directions passed by the Supreme Court while deciding the matter afresh. The order suffers from no illegality and rather in fact is absolutely in tune with the directions of the Supreme Court . . .'[2] In November, the Supreme Court dismissed a petition against the order to try Bholu as an adult.[3]

Just as the juvenile vs adult question has been knocked from one court to the next so was the question of whether Bholu should be given bail. 'Default bail' is bail given because the investigating authority, whether it be the police or the CBI, has not filed charges within the stipulated period of time. Bholu's father applied for default bail in the JJB, then in the district children's and women's sessions court, then in the sessions court, then in the Punjab and Haryana High Court and finally in the Supreme Court between December 2017 and July 2018. The CBI, and Prince's family, opposed the bail plea at each stage.

Bholu's father argues, 'The CBI failed to file the charge sheet within sixty days of taking him into custody. My son was apprehended late night on 7 November and the CBI filed a partial charge sheet . . . on 4 February. There is no evidence against him,' the father said.

'Tareekh pe Tareekh'

But Bholu has been denied default bail by all the courts up to the apex level.[4] According to various orders passed by the Supreme Court, if an accused can be punished with death, life imprisonment or with imprisonment of ten years or more, the investigation agency has an extended period of ninety days to file the charge sheet.[5]

Then Bholu's father started applying for 'regular bail' starting October 2018 in the JJB. 'The theory of the CBI is baseless and my son has been framed. The judiciary must watch it (the CCTV footage) before announcing any decision or before rejecting the bail,' Bholu's father said. The parents said the extensive media coverage in the case was the main reason behind the courts rejecting their son's bail application. But like in the case of Bholu's default bail, each level of court, starting with the JJB, has denied Bholu regular bail too. Bholu's 'regular bail' plea had been pending before the Punjab and Haryana High Court for more than a year and a half when on 30 June 2020 the high court also rejected Bholu's bail plea.

After much back and forth, Bholu was finally granted interim bail by the Supreme Court in October 2022, three days after the JJB ordered him to be tried as an adult.[6] In total, Bholu had applied for bail at least 21 times since 2017.

It is not just on the questions of bail and Bholu's juvenile vs adult status that the two sides moved applications and appeals, but on a range of other issues too: getting certified copies of Bholu's statements as recorded by the JJB, the process of obtaining Bholu's fingerprints and even on the question of where Bholu is staying.

Indeed, early on in the process, in January 2018 itself, the additional sessions judge Jasbir Singh Kundu, perhaps fatigued by the sheer number of motions, imposed a fine of Rs 21,000 on Bholu's father for 'wasting the court's time'.

'The conduct of the appellant (accused) indicates that he is taking the court proceedings for a joyride. He has indulged in wasting precious court time in baseless litigation on account of which seven court hearings have gone down the drain.'

The court came down heavily on Bholu's father and conjectured that he was attempting to delay the investigations so that default bail could then be obtained.

Judge Kundu further remarked, 'The applicant, himself an advocate by profession, is hereby warned that in case he indulges in such activities of repeating prayers which have already been declined, these attempts would be considered as putting the court intentionally in the dark and not only would the prayers be declined with heavy costs but strictures would be passed against the applicant regarding his conduct,' read the order.[7]

One point of contention between Bholu's father and the court has been on the issue of where Bholu will be held. Till his eighteenth birthday in April 2019, Bholu was staying at the observation home in Faridabad. But after he turned eighteen, the JJB recommended that he be moved to a home called Place of Safety in Madhuban, Karnal. This is apparently a routine matter as the Karnal home is specifically a place where eighteen- to twenty-one-year-olds are held, whereas the Faridabad home is for under-eighteens only. Dinesh Yadav, superintendent of the Faridabad observation home where Bholu had been staying till then, had requested the JJB to shift him to Place of Safety. According to Yadav, Bholu was very aggressive with his co-residents – though this has nothing to do with Bholu being moved, which was a routine matter. Yadav also said that Bholu was sad when he left. He was attached to his friends at the Faridabad home.[8]

Bholu's father first challenged this move in the JJB itself and then in the sessions court. He protested that 'Place of Safety in Madhuban, Karnal is nearly 170 kilometres from Gurugram, and it will be difficult travelling all that way once a week to meet my son. It will also be tiring for him to appear before the Juvenile Justice Board every fourteen days.' His appeals were, however, turned down by both courts.

But, troublingly, while the sessions court appeal was ongoing, the principal magistrate of the JJB, Manglesh Kumar Choubey, wrote to the sessions judge informing him that Bholu's father was trying to get him to withdraw the original order to shift his son.

He told the judge that a former bar council president of Gurugram and the current bar council secretary of Gurugram had approached him along with Bholu's father. 'I was astonished to see that they were trying to influence me to withdraw my order ... They were pressuring me not to shift the juvenile ... I found the tone of the juvenile's father to be threatening,' the JJB magistrate wrote.[9]

Bholu's father denies these charges. 'I never threatened the principal magistrate. This is a wrong and baseless allegation against me,' he said.

'Tareekh pe Tareekh'

Sushil Tekriwal, counsel for the father of the victim, said that the sessions court has rightly dismissed Bholu's appeal. 'There has already been a delay in the court proceedings and the trial of the case is yet to begin. Such hurdles affect court cases and end up harassing the deceased's family. The father is running from pillar to post to get justice, but justice is getting delayed due to such petitions,' he said.

In fact, Bhaskar wants the case to be transferred out of Gurugram as he believes Bholu's father is interfering in the proceedings there. The CBI has also filed a petition before the Punjab and Haryana High Court seeking a transfer of the trial out of Gurugram to the special CBI court in Panchkula.

These aren't the only petitions on Bhaskar's radar. With one hand he's fighting the family of the accused and with the other he's duelling with the school and its management. For instance, on 12 July 2018, Bhaskar Thakkar filed a petition in the Punjab and Haryana High Court for the disaffiliation of the school. The high court observed that a fact-finding committee should be appointed by the CBSE on the issue of disaffiliation of the school for multiple lapses. The allegation is that Prince was killed due to the negligence of the Gurugram school management and the lack of safety and security measures. While the CBSE's energies to see this process through seem to have flagged, this petition is still alive in the court.

13

Road to the Trial

In January 2023, the Gurugram special children's court framed murder charges against Bholu, paving the way for his trial. Taking into consideration the evidence, additional district and sessions judge Tarun Singal found him prima facie guilty of murder under Section 302 (murder) of the Indian Penal Code. The court, while framing charges, asked Bholu whether he wanted to face trial or plead guilty, to which he replied that he was ready to face trial.[1]

The CBI was directed to produce the witnesses at the next hearing scheduled for 20 February.

The Thakkars' counsel, Sushil Tekriwal, said the development indicated that the case would be fast-tracked and the trial concluded expeditiously.

Bhaskar felt his prayers had been finally answered.

CBI prosecutor Amit Jindal contends there is

enough evidence against Bholu. 'He committed cold-blooded murder in a well-planned manner and tried to destroy evidence at the scene of the crime and later searched online for ways to clean fingerprints off the school bathroom walls.'

Finally, five years and five months after Prince's death, Bholu was tried as an adult on 20 February, 2023 at the district and sessions court.[2]

The CBI, in its charge sheet, listed 127 witnesses – including teachers, students, police, visitors, cybercrime teams, forensic experts and others. The central probe agency has also mentioned the history of internet searches, in the days prior to the murder, that was retrieved from Bholu's laptop. The searches ranged from 'ways to remove fingerprints' to 'effects of various kinds of poison on the human body', among others.

On the first day of trial, the prosecution examined two witnesses, including forensic expert Dr Deepak Mathur, who had conducted Prince's post-mortem examination. He was quizzed on the finer details of the weapon. 'The public prosecutor asked my opinion regarding the weapon. All the parcels (containing evidence) that were sealed after the murder were opened in the court. We have already given our report after the post mortem examination, which mentions the injuries, condition of the body, cause of death, distance between injuries and portable time between injury and death,' he said. However, his testimony remained incomplete on the day due to time constraints and he was asked to return on 3 March for cross-examination by the defence counsel.

Dr B.K. Mohapatra, principal scientific officer of the Central Forensic Science Laboratory, was also examined. He had carried out the serological examination of the material objects and evidence in the case, such as the crime weapon (knife), clothes of the accused on the day of the incident, etc.

As the months wore on, the list of witnesses examined by the court slowly increased to 14; however, in July 2023, one of the witnesses unexpectedly turned hostile.[3] Pankaj, the owner of the Sohna shop from where Bholu allegedly bought the knife, refused to identify Bholu as a customer, saying he could not be sure because he had sold several similar knives, and such knives were sold in other shops as well.

To be sure, the CBI, after detaining Bholu in 2017 and before filing the charge sheet in 2018, had already examined 19 witnesses in the case. These witnesses, in case they turn hostile now, are liable to face legal action.

On 19 August, the trial court directed the CBI to seek dates at closer intervals or get more witnesses to the stand at each hearing, expressing concern about the slow progress thus far.[4]

Additional sessions judge Tarun Singhal noted that only one or two hearings were taking place in a month and two witnesses were listed by the CBI for recording statements at each hearing. The judge said he will change the timing of the hearings to accommodate more witnesses. The court directed all subsequent hearings to begin at 11am, as opposed to 2 p.m. thus far, on each date. He asked the CBI to bring three witnesses to record statements at the next hearing in September.

14

Three Families

The only person with the same energy and hope for justice is the helpless father of the victim. Bhaskar wakes up every morning and fights to ensure justice for his little boy. It's a tiring and lonely – and expensive – fight.

Bhaskar says, 'It is not easy. I have been running from one court to another. Most people tend to give up the battle halfway. But I'm determined ... for every hearing, the monetary expense is yet another factor. No wonder people who can't afford the expenses accept whatever they get.'

'I now understand why people give up court battles halfway. It is not an easy task to fight a case from a lower court to the Supreme Court,' he adds, feeling powerless. Nearly three years after the murder, the Thakkar family haven't even crossed the first hurdle of the battle as the trial is yet to begin.[1]

Even though Bhaskar's employers have been understanding of his situation, juggling court dates for hearings in Gurugram, Delhi and Chandigarh has not been easy. 'My savings are over and most of my salary is being spent in the legal battle. Also, I hardly have any time to spend with my family because I keep running around for the case.'

Prince's perfectly ironed school uniforms and polished black shoes, his sports shoes with splotches of mud on them, his numerous toys and the pictures he drew with crayons are arranged neatly in his wardrobe, left exactly as they were the day he died. Prince's broken mother has not given any of his things away. 'When people ask me how we have coped with the situation, I tell them that we are lost without our son,' she shared.

'I see him everywhere, every day. His clothes, lunch box, stationery items – everything reminds me of him. From the day I conceived him until the day he died, I remember each and every thing he did,' says Jaya. 'I open the cupboard but do not touch his belongings, I just stand or sit on the floor, looking at his drawings,' she adds.

Tears roll down Prince's father's cheeks as he remembers their last goodbye, the last day he dropped his son to school in his car. Bhaskar says he still spends nights sobbing for his innocent son.

'Not a day goes by that I don't think of my son when I cross these lanes. Whenever I see the general store he loved, his school lane or his friends cycling by, my eyes invariably search for him. I often go up to the terrace and think of the times he would drag me upstairs to watch the planes fly by,' Bhaskar recalls.

Prince's parents have set up a trust in his name, with the objectives of fighting for justice for him, so that such an incident does not take place anywhere in the country again, and to work towards the safety, welfare and well-being of children.

The couple obviously withdrew their daughter from the Gurugram school immediately after the incident. Some other schools had offered to provide her admission and free education up to class twelve. But Bhaskar turned them down as he did not want a 'free offer' from anyone.

The couple was blessed with a baby girl on 13 June 2020 in Gurugram after trying for two years. 'We've been visiting doctors for over two years; my wife underwent treatment,' Bhaskar says, referring to the tubectomy Jaya had to get reversed.

At times Bhaskar feels a rush of anger. Years of

pain for the family are the result of 'the few seconds of misery my son must have gone through before leaving us forever'.

'When I first saw Bholu in the CBI headquarters, the boy had no idea of the pain and suffering he had caused. When I watch him in court, I feel pity for him as his family is still behaving normally and assuring him that they will save him. Not once has the family expressed sympathy or apologized. The juvenile responsible for Prince's death must be held accountable,' says Bhaskar.[2]

Who could blame the Thakkars if the confidence they felt for the CBI in the early days of the investigation starts waning. The Thakkar family lawyer, Sushil Tekriwal, is dismayed that 'the final charge sheet against the [Gurugram] Police and the school management is yet to be filed'. What the Thakkars need more than anything is the patience and the stamina to see the legal battle through – and money to pay their hefty legal bills. Peace of mind is more elusive. The family has been through more hardship in three years than most people have to endure in a lifetime.

Three Families

For Bholu and his family, the past three years have been difficult. The boy who had all manner of creature comforts now lives in a dingy room with other juveniles. His bail applications have been repeatedly rejected; he and his family have faced some form of 'social rejection' too. His younger brother has been subjected to a lot of discrimination. He has stopped going out to play and often complains that other children do not treat him well at school.[3]

Bholu's mother has been in a state of despair ever since Bholu was apprehended. And while Bholu's father says they haven't lost hope and still believe their son will soon be with them, there is a long battle ahead, one that has not even started yet. 'My son keeps asking me when he can get out of the juvenile home. I feel helpless as I am fighting the battle to save him. I know he has been framed by the CBI,' the father says, adding his son would have been in college now had he been free.

The boy's father has received a copy of the CCTV footage based on which Bholu was apprehended. He argues that if the footage is to be considered as evidence, his son should be acquitted. He said there is no such footage where Bholu is seen walking alongside Prince with his hand on his shoulder.

These are matters for the court to decide. For now, in the eyes of the law, Bholu is innocent until declared guilty. The sooner the case is decided, the better for Bholu and for the Thakkars.

~

One would think this is a happy ending for Amit Kumar and his family at least, and it is in a way. Amit Kumar was arrested for Prince's murder on 8 September 2017, the day of the killing itself. He was granted bail in November 2017 after spending seventy-four days in jail. And he was acquitted of all charges in February 2018. But even though Amit was acquitted in this brutal murder case, life continued to be unkind to him.

The stigma of being an accused in a case of murder and paedophilia is hard to shake off. He was dismissed from service by the Gurugram school. And even though the public seems convinced of his innocence, no one was ready to help him out when it came to giving him a job that could sustain him and his family. He approached various schools and agencies for employment opportunities, but he was turned down under some pretext or the other. Amit initially had to make do with a few odd jobs he got here and there. He even started a small vegetable shop but had to shut it down for lack of funds. He has worked as a cleaner at a mall in Badshahpur where he would earn Rs 6500 a month for an eight-hour shift. It's hard to make ends meet and educate his children. The latest is that he works as a watchman at a mall.

His reputation seems to follow him everywhere. 'People sympathize with me but do not want to offer me a job,' he says. Anil, Kumar's father, said that the family had considered relocating but they don't have the means to do that. He said he wants to go some place new where they won't be asked so many questions or looked at suspiciously.

Ironically, Amit wants his children to become policemen when they grow up. 'My wife and I work hard to ensure our sons' education is not affected. I want them to study hard and join the police force, so people get justice,' he says.

When he is not at work Amit prefers to stay at home, help his wife cook and spend time with his two sons. Kumar's wife Mala works at a private school and manages the family's finances. She says that even though her husband has been acquitted, her children have a difficult time. 'Our children have gone through a lot due to the arrest. Their classmates mock them and constantly ask why their father was arrested, but I am unable to tell them anything,' she says.

Kumar's role in the case is not over yet – he is now the CBI's prime witness. Kumar said he is grateful to the victim's family for having faith in him and believing he wasn't the murderer. 'I pray that justice is served,' Kumar says.

Three years after the incident, the alleged torture he faced at the hands of the Gurugram Police is still fresh in his mind. 'I am still unable to lead a normal life and sometimes get up in the middle of the night and wonder why I had to suffer so much for no fault of mine,' he says. The mere recollection of what he went through makes him shudder. 'I was arrested, tortured and brutally assaulted in the lock-up in their efforts to make me confess to the crime,' he says. 'These days I just keep to myself,' Kumar adds.

Mala insists she will never forgive the police officers involved in her husband's arrest and those who allegedly tortured and framed him.

The fact that Amit was tortured and framed is now widely believed, though why the Gurugram Police would do such a thing is still unclear. Were they working on the directions of someone else whom they were protecting? Or was this just a case of finding a voiceless scapegoat for the crime to deflect the intense criticism from the press?

The National Human Rights Commission (NHRC) even ordered the Gurugram Police to pay a compensation of Rs 1 lakh to Amit Kumar in February 2018. But Amit refused to accept the compensation, terming it inadequate. 'I was tortured, beaten, hung upside down and my head submerged in water by the police to get me to confess. I was asked to parade before the media and they humiliated me in front of my family and public. The incident still haunts me in my sleep,' he says. Were it not for the fact that his name was sullied and dragged through the mud, Amit says he would have taken the money which he would have used to construct a bathroom in his house.

But for the moment, he needs justice, he says. 'I was subjected to third-degree torture despite revealing all information and the sequence of events to CBI officials.[4] I was framed by the senior officials to save the juvenile who is now behind bars. I need action against those who were involved,' says Kumar.

The CBI IO Ajay Kumar Bassi had submitted a 279-page draft supplementary charge sheet internally to the CBI on 7 September 2018 and recommended prosecution against four officers, including the SHO of Bhondsi, who was the IO in the case. The CBI finally filed an 80-odd-page supplementary charge sheet in court in January 2021.[5] The charge sheet named four Gurugram police officers – Brihm Singh, then assistant commissioner of police; Narender Khatana, then SHO of Bhondsi police station; Inspector Shamsher Singh, then IO of the case; Subhash, exempted assistant sub-inspector – for falsely implicating Amit Kumar and for fabricating documents against him in 2017. Bassi was removed as the IO of the case at the end of September 2018.

'The four officers who have been mentioned in the CBI's supplementary charge sheet should be punished. I am waiting for them to see how it feels when you are humiliated in public,' Kumar says.

In February 2021, the CBI court of Haryana pulled up the state government and the state police, accusing them of 'sleeping like Kumbhakarna' instead of discharging their statutory duties.[6]

'The accused four police officials virtually made life hell for Amit Kumar and put his entire family on the brink of starvation. The incident gave a bad name to him in society and put a blot on his career, which will take time to vanish. The best solace for this person in the scenario will be that accused persons who were responsible for his plight should face prosecution and the law should take its course, but to my utter surprise, the concerned sanctioning authorities are sitting upon the request of sanction,' the court observed in its order.

Inspector Narender Khatana, the SHO who had arrested Kumar on 8 September, said the allegations against him are baseless. 'He was arrested from the school after bloodstains were spotted on his shirt. The preliminary investigations revealed that Kumar was guilty and he had confessed to the crime.'

Even if one were to overlook the issue of torture, the sloppiness of the Gurugram Police's investigation is undeniable. These could also be signs of a cover-up and evidence tampering. There is a cloud of doubt on whether the case diaries that were supposed to have been written out on the day of the murder were indeed written then or filled out later.

There are questions on whether Amit's clothes were seized on 8 September 2017 as is claimed by the police. Chirag Goti, a correspondent of Aaj Tak news channel, interviewed Kumar in the same clothes on 9 September.

The CCTV footage was shown to the schoolteachers

by SHO Khatana on 18 September 2017, but in the police record it says this was done on 11 September. A number of teachers have confirmed this as well as the fact that no inquiries were made by SHO Khatana on 18 September 2017 about Bholu – in spite of the fact that Bholu's alibi, Tarun, had plainly denied meeting him or planning to meet him that morning.

Kumar, who currently works as a security guard at a mall, says he's living hand-to-mouth, and still gets threats from police officers, ordering him to withdraw his case.

The alleged motive or mastermind of the alleged framing and torture is still unknown.

15

The School

When the school reopened, it had a new administration and a full-time safety and security officer in place. But by then many of the parents had withdrawn their children from the school. Sameer, the father of a class two student, was one of them. 'I decided to withdraw my son from the school shortly after the incident. This was the second incident in the same group of schools and I was scared. I knew nothing much would change,' he said.

Kajal, a parenting coach and a counselling expert who volunteered to be part of a team of psychologists that would counsel the school's students and their parents, said most of them were worried about such an incident occurring again. 'They accused the school administration of failing to ensure security on premises. They had many questions – these ranged from "why was there no bolt and lock on the door of some of the bathroom cubicles?" to "why was there no frisking or checking of ID cards at the entrance?"' she said.[1]

'After the incident, CCTV cameras and security guards were added for increased safety. Metal detectors were installed to frisk those entering the school,' said a school official.

Eventually the boundary wall, which was broken earlier, was also constructed. Almost a week after the incident, the CBSE issued new security guidelines to be implemented by affiliated institutions, failing which they would be derecognized. The board mandated safety audits, installation of CCTV cameras, police verification and psychometric evaluation of staff and the constitution of parent–teacher–student committees. It stated that access to school buildings by outsiders should be controlled and visitors monitored. Other schools in Gurugram and the rest of the country followed suit. They beefed up security by adding CCTV cameras and restricting outsiders from entering the premises.

Sudha Goyal, the director of Scottish High International School in Sushant Lok-2, said, 'The school has been a part of various government audits.[2]

We have augmented security at the peripheries, increased camera surveillance and hired additional resident doctors and nurses. The school also holds frequent counselling for students and the staff.' Goyal said every employee has gone through a complete background check.

Aparna Erry, principal, DAV Public School, sector 14, Gurugram, has mandated that parents and guardians have to carry a pass while dropping and picking up their wards.[3]

Teachers in schools across the city said the incident led to a trust deficit between schools and parents, and it took more than a year to overcome this. 'The incident led to unrest. It caused a rift among the stakeholders,' said Neeti Kaushik, principal of Mount Olympus School in sector 47, Gurugram.[4]

In the last five years, most private schools in the city have started taking steps to train their staff and students to keep vigil and monitor any concern. Saloni, a member of the safety committee that was set up in the district after the incident, said schools have been regularly sharing updates on all and any type of safety controls being added to the system.[5] 'Parents are informed about any hiring of female guards for buses, training of their support staff or tightening movement of parents in the school during working days ... barricading of out-of-bounds areas for kids and visitors are seen in the schools,' she said.

But parents still have questions and doubts. Tripti Singh Rathore, a resident of sector 61 and administrator of the Facebook group Gurgaon Parents for Better Education, said, 'Private cabs and autos still ferry children in large numbers with complete impunity. We see school buses without any names on them. All the changes after the incident seem like an eyewash.'[6]

Neela Kaushik, a Gurugram-based parent and founder of the Facebook group GurgaonMoms, said that for any effective change, the whole system needs to be addressed. 'For a change to happen, the largest and biggest stakeholder – the parents – need to become more vigilant.'[7]

After the incident took place, the administration had made promises to pull up schools, conduct regular checks and ensure that all schools follow safety and security guidelines, but there has been no strategy to enforce this. Schools have had no surprise checks.

Some parents still have nightmares: are we waiting for yet another gruesome episode to take place? But on cooler reflection one realizes that even if many of the proposed changes are put in place – ID cards for parents, areas where only students are permitted, building of boundary walls, guards on buses, background checks of employees, separate bathrooms for students, etc. – an incident like this might still have taken place. Could we be focusing on the wrong things?

Indeed, where many parents and the media have focused on certain alleged lapses of the school and the school's culpability, Bassi says that in the detailed investigation conducted by the CBI, they did not find the school to be responsible for what had happened.[8] While Bhaskar Thakkar feels deeply upset that the school administration and the owners got away scot-free in the CBI charge sheet, Bassi finds blaming the school to be baseless and felt that the school administration was put under a lot of undue stress.[9]

For instance, many people wrongly thought that the CCTV cameras in the school were not working. But, in fact, fifteen out of sixteen cameras were operational. Similarly, many people wondered why the staff and the children used the same washroom. But if the CBI theory that Bholu committed the murder is correct then this question is irrelevant to begin with. Besides, there were no authoritative guidelines on this issue.

Bassi clarified that the northern zone head and group HR head of the school's parent group were mere employees and had no role to play in this murder. While this is an unpopular view, Bassi says the school was being blamed for a lot of issues it simply had no control over.[10]

Bassi is partly right: many people were focusing on the wrong things. But if the CBI theory that Bholu committed the crime is correct, then perhaps this shows us that what we need most of all is for parents and schools to take mental illness and behavioural problem signs seriously. That, to my mind, is the bigger takeaway from this awful episode, and we should be asking why the Gurugram school missed so many critical warning signs. According to the CBI, Bholu wanted to get away from the exams and the PTA meeting which is why he committed the murder. But, going by the account in the charge sheet, this wasn't a bolt from the blue. There was a gradual build-up to this point which should have been spotted and treated.

Take, for instance, the assertion of Bholu's friend in the charge sheet that one time when Bholu was in class nine he consumed poison (and blamed someone else for this), or the assertion in the charge sheet that because of some 'obnoxious substance in his water bottle' he was unable to sit for his exams and had to be hospitalized for a few days in 2016. The school nurse, Manika Govind, told Nisha Saini that at least on one occasion Bholu had consumed alcohol on the school premises. Several of his teachers while talking to Nisha Saini mentioned that Bholu used to shout at other students frequently. He was allegedly a rule breaker who used a mobile phone on campus.[11] So the real question we should be asking is, if all that the CBI is claiming is accurate, why didn't these incidents raise red flags for the school? Do these incidents taken together not indicate that Bholu needed help, counselling, guidance of some kind? Bholu's mother is not wrong when she asks sceptically: if everything that the CBI says is correct then why did the school not raise these behavioural issues earlier?[12]

According to Bholu's schoolmates, there were other warning signs too that the school seems to have missed totally. Once Bholu added a poisonous substance in the water bottle of a girl who sat on the front bench of the class. It was a stroke of good luck that she did not drink from the bottle because there were fumes coming out of it.

Bholu's friends mentioned incidents where he inflicted injuries on his arm to impress a girl or to emotionally blackmail her. They said that Bholu was starved for attention and that he could be domineering and bullying.

According to some other students, Bholu sometimes paid his classmates to do his homework. Bholu's father gave him adequate pocket money and he even used to ride around on a motorbike. His parents rarely refused him anything.[13]

Dr Amit Sen, an expert in child and adolescent mental health, studied the case files deeply. He said that if the CBI's version of events was correct, Bholu might have been suffering from depression. Such adolescents may exhibit sorrow or sadness, and they can at times be aggressive. Dr Sen certainly feels that the school and Bholu's family should have read these signs. Children who are depressed or have behavioural issues need help and assistance, which only schools and parents can and should offer. So even if the worst of what the CBI claims about Bholu was correct, was he not a victim himself then? More than merely obsessing over CCTVs, how about we get serious about mental health in our schools?

But this is an inconvenient, long-term solution that

doesn't lend itself to being converted into a rule or a guideline that can be issued as a government circular and implemented on pain of penalty. It's far easier to buy the peace and create the illusion of safety and action by saying you need to have separate toilets for school staff or some such thing.

∼

As his trial progresses, Bholu, now 22, is a busy man. While his teenaged self wanted to study law, he is now content to pursue another course via correspondence.

It remains to be seen how long the trial will take and how the scales of justice will weigh the myriad evidences in the case. But there are no winners here. Prince has lost his life. Bhaskar and Jaya have lost their son. Bholu and Amit Kumar have lost their futures. The Gurugram school has lost its reputation. The Gurugram Police have lost all credibility.

Notes

Prologue: Blood Tracks

1. Interview with Harjot on 8 September 2017 in Bhondsi.
2. Author saw the bloodstained knife lying in the commode on 8 September 2017.
   Interview with a student who saw the knife.
   The physical education teacher had seen the knife in the commode and recorded his statements before the CBI officials on 21 December 2017 and 17 January 2018.
3. CBI charge sheet: As per pages 10 and 11, paragraphs 24 and 25.
   Interview with Harjot on 8 September 2017.
   Interview with the school coordinator and Jairaj (school bus driver) on 8 September 2017.
4. Interview with Bhaskar Thakkar (Prince's father) on 8 September 2017 at the mortuary.
5. CBI charge sheet: As per page 5, paragraph 7.
   Interview with the school coordinator at the school on 8 September 2017.

Notes

1. The Phone Call

1. Interview with Bhaskar Thakkar and Jaya Thakkar on 12 October 2017 at their residence.
2. Interview with Bhaskar Thakkar on 8 September 2017 at the police headquarters in Gurugram.
3. CBI charge sheet: As per page 5, paragraph 3. This is the statement recorded by the school receptionist at the CBI headquarters in Delhi on 10 January 2018.
4. CBI charge sheet: As per pages 4 and 5, paragraph 3. Interview with Bhaskar Thakkar on 8 September 2017 at the police headquarters in Gurugram.
5. Interview with Bhaskar Thakkar on 8 September 2017 at the police headquarters in Gurugram.
6. Ibid.
   Interview with the school coordinator on 8 September 2017 and interview with the neighbours on 8 September 2017.
7. CBI charge sheet: As per page 6, paragraph 8.
8. Interview with Bhaskar Thakkar and Jaya Thakkar on 8 September 2017.
9. Author was present at the Thakkars' residence on 8 September 2017.
10. Ibid.
11. Interview with the school coordinator and the principal in the school premises on 8 September 2017.
12. Interview with the Thakkars' neighbours in Shyam Kunj on 8 September 2017.
13. Several interviews with the IO of the CBI, Ajay Kumar Bassi, who said the teachers had recorded their statements regarding the incident (20 December 2017, 15 January 2018 and 21 May 2018).

2. The First Arrest

1. Statement by the school receptionist, recorded at the CBI headquarters on 10 January 2018. It is attached with the CBI charge sheet.
2. Ibid.
   Statement by the parent of a student in the same school. His statement was recorded on 17 January 2018 at the CBI headquarters.
3. Author was present in the school on 8 September 2017.
4. Ibid.
   CBI charge sheet: As per page 15, paragraph 39. Statements of the following people were recorded by the CBI: Tarun, a student, on 28 October 2017; the physical education teacher, on 21 December 2017; Deepali, the teacher who was present in Bholu's class on 8 September, on 28 November 2017.
5. CBI charge sheet: As per document D15.
6. As per the school maid/cleaner's statement recorded by the CBI at the CBI headquarters on 17 January 2018.
7. CBI charge sheet: As per page 5 of document D36.
8. As per the CCTV footage recovered by the Gurugram Police and the CBI.
9. CBI charge sheet: As per page 12, paragraph 29.
10. Interview with Amit Kumar at his residence in Ghamroj village on 21 and 22 November 2017.
11. Interview with the school coordinator and the acting principal on 8 September 2017 at the school.
12. Interview with the school coordinator on 8 September 2017 at the school.

3. The Post-Mortem

1. Interview with Dr Deepak Mathur on 8, 9 and 10 September 2017.
2. CBI charge sheet: As per page 4, paragraph 2 of document D2.
3. Interview with Dr Deepak Mathur on 8 and 9 September 2017 at the mortuary in Gurugram.
4. Interview with Dr Deepak Mathur on 9 and 10 September 2017.
   CBI charge sheet: As per page 20, paragraph 49.
5. Post-mortem report (CBI charge sheet): As per page 20, paragraph 49 of document D42 (four pages).
6. Interview with Dr Deepak Mathur on 8 and 10 September, 12 October and 11 December 2017.
7. CBI charge sheet: As per page 20, paragraph 49.
   Interview with Dr Deepak Mathur on 9 September 2017.

4. The Press Conference

1. Author was present at the mortuary.
2. DCP Deepak Saharan was present in the police building and met the family members when they arrived to meet the police commissioner on 8 September 2017.
   Author was present with the father at the police commissioner's office.
3. Interview with Bhaskar Thakkar and his brother Varun Chandra Thakkar.
   Interview with DCP Deepak Saharan on 8 September 2017.

Notes

4. Author was present with the family members on 8 September 2017.
5. Interview with Mala, Amit's wife, on 9 September 2017 at Ghamroj village.
6. Ibid.
7. Interview with Mala and her father-in-law on 8, 12, 13 and 14 September 2017 at Ghamroj village.
8. Interview with Chirag Gothi, journalist at Aaj Tak, at Sohna police station on 9 September 2017. The interview was aired on Aaj Tak the same day.
9. Interview with Mala on 9 September 2017 at Ghamroj village.
10. Interview with Mala at Ghamroj village on 9 September 2017.
11. CBI charge sheet: As per page 12, paragraph 30. Amit Kumar's statement recorded on 30 November 2017 at the CBI office and at the Saket court under section 164 of the Code of Criminal Procedure (CrPC).
    Interview with Amit on 21 November 2017 at his residence in Ghamroj village.
12. Interview with Mala and Amit's paternal uncle on 15 September 2017.
13. CCTV footage record filed in CBI charge sheet Annexure A (four pages).
14. Interview with Ajay Kumar Bassi, IO of the CBI, on 28 February 2018.
15. CBI charge sheet: As per page 3 of document D16.
    Several interviews with IO Ajay Kumar Bassi on 20 December 2017, 15 January 2018 and 21 May 2018.

Notes

16. Interview with DCP Sumit Kuhar and DCP Ashok Bakshi on 9 September 2017.
17. Interview with Jaya Thakkar on 9 September 2017 at the Thakkar residence.
18. Interview with Jaya Thakkar on 8 September 2017 at the Thakkar residence.
19. Interview with public prosecutor Anurag Hooda on 5 March 2018.
20. CBI charge sheet: As per page 5, paragraph 4.

5. The Cremation

1. Interview with Bhaskar Thakkar, his brother Varun Thakkar and wife Jaya Thakkar on 9 and 10 September 2017.

6. The Handover

1. Interview with Mohit Verma, advocate of Amit Kumar, on 11 September 2017 at Amit's residence in Ghamroj village.
2. Interview with Mohit Verma on 12 September 2017.
3. Interview with Bhaskar Thakkar on 8 November 2017.
4. Ibid.
5. Court order dated 28 February 2018 passed by the additional sessions judge, J.S. Kundu, Gurugram.

7. The CBI

1. As per the CBI sources.
2. As per the school's CCTV footage. This was filed in Annexure A of the CBI charge sheet against Bholu on 5 February 2018 in the Gurugram court.

Notes

Note: The CCTV cameras were running twenty-three minutes behind actual time as per the statements of employees of the company that installed the CCTV cameras, which were recorded by the CBI on 8 January 2018 and filed with the CBI charge sheet.

3. CBI charge sheet: As per page 15, paragraph 38.
4. CBI charge sheet: As per page 15, paragraph 38, filed on 5 February 2018 and as per Annexure A of the charge sheet.
5. Ibid.
6. As per Annexure A of the CBI charge sheet filed in the court on 5 February 2018.
7. Ibid.
8. As per page 74 of Annexure A of the CBI charge sheet filed in the court on 5 February 2018.

    CBI charge sheet: As per pages 10 and 11, paragraph 25.

    CBI charge sheet: As per page 12, paragraphs 28 and 29.

    As per Harjot's (the gardener) statement recorded by the CBI on 27 December 2017 at the CBI office, New Delhi, and filed with the CBI charge sheet.

    As per Jairaj's (the driver) statement recorded by the CBI on 30 November 2017 at the CBI office, New Delhi, and filed with the CBI charge sheet.

    As per Amit Kumar's statement recorded by the CBI on 30 November 2017 at the CBI office, New Delhi, and filed with the CBI charge sheet.

9. CBI charge sheet: As per page 15, paragraph 38, and as per Annexure A filed with the CBI charge sheet.

    He entered the school from the wooden gate at 7.58.04 a.m., exited the washroom gallery at 7.58.51 a.m. and then re-entered it at 7.59.03 a.m. He was then seen exiting the washroom gallery with Prince at 8.00.34 a.m.

Notes

10. CBI charge sheet: As per document 205. Bholu's statement was recorded by SHO Narender Khatana on 15 September 2017. The same is mentioned on page 40 of the list of documents in the CBI charge sheet.

    As per Bholu's statement recorded at the Gurugram court on the request of the Gurugram Police on 19 September 2017, which is filed with the CBI charge sheet as document 205. The same is mentioned on page 40 of the list of documents in the CBI charge sheet.

    CBI charge sheet: As per page 13, paragraph 33.

11. CBI charge sheet: As per page 13, paragraph 33.

    CBI charge sheet: As per document 205. Bholu's statement was recorded by SHO Narender Khatana on 15 September 2017. The same is mentioned on page 40 of the list of documents in the CBI charge sheet.

    As per Bholu's statement recorded at the Gurugram court on the request of the Gurugram Police on 19 September 2017, which is filed with the CBI charge sheet as document 205. The same is mentioned on page 40 of the list of documents in the CBI charge sheet.

12. CBI charge sheet: As per page 10, paragraph 25.

    CBI charge sheet: As per page 13, paragraph 33.

    CBI charge sheet: As per pages 13 and 14, paragraph 35. CBI charge sheet: As per document 205. Bholu's statement was recorded by SHO Narender Khatana on 15 September 2017. The same is mentioned on page 40 of the list of documents in the CBI charge sheet.

    As per Bholu's statement recorded at the Gurugram court on the request of the Gurugram Police on 19 September 2017, which is filed with the CBI charge sheet as document 205.

The same is mentioned on page 40 of the list of documents in the CBI charge sheet.

CBI charge sheet: As per page 15, paragraph 38.

CBI charge sheet: As per Annexure A containing four pages documenting the movement of Amit, Bholu, Tarun, Harjot, Prince (the deceased).

13. CBI charge sheet: As per page 13, paragraph 33.

    CBI charge sheet: As per document 205. Bholu's statement was recorded by SHO Narender Khatana on 15 September 2017. The same is mentioned on page 40 of the list of documents in the CBI charge sheet.

    As per Bholu's statement recorded at the Gurugram court on the request of the Gurugram Police on 19 September 2017, which is filed with the CBI charge sheet as document 205. The same is mentioned on page 40 of the list of documents in the CBI charge sheet.

14. CBI charge sheet: As per page 25, paragraph 62.

    CBI charge sheet: As per document 142-B of the list of documents in the charge sheet filed on 5 February 2018.

    CBI charge sheet: As per the statements of fifteen teachers recorded on 23 December 2017 at the CBI office, New Delhi.

    CBI charge sheet: As per the statements of the independent witnesses recorded by the CBI on 23 December 2017 at the CBI office.

15. CBI charge sheet: As per page 13, paragraph 34.

16. CBI charge sheet: As per page 24, paragraph 60.

    CBI charge sheet: As per pages 25 and 26, paragraph 64. As per documents 65, 67 and 68 of the list of documents filed by the CBI along with the CBI charge sheet against Bholu.

17. CBI charge sheet: As per page 13, paragraph 34.
18. Several interviews with Ajay Kumar Bassi on 20 December 2017, 15 January 2018 and 21 May 2018.
19. Ibid.
20. CBI charge sheet: As per page 13, paragraph 34.
21. CBI charge sheet: As per pages 13 and 14, paragraph 35.
    CBI charge sheet: As per Tarun's statement recorded by the CBI on 28 October 2017 at the BSF Campus, Sohna Road, Gurugram. This was filed with the CBI charge sheet.
    CBI charge sheet: As per page 15, paragraph 38.
    CBI charge sheet: As per Annexure A of the charge sheet filed on 5 February 2018 in the Gurugram court.

8. The Evidence

1. CBI charge sheet: As per page 5, paragraph 6.
   CBI charge sheet: As per Amit Kumar's statement recorded by the CBI on 30 November 2017 at the CBI office, New Delhi, and filed with the CBI charge sheet.
2. CBI charge sheet: As per page 15, paragraph 38. As per analysis of Annexure A filed by the CBI along with the charge sheet which shows the movement of various persons, especially Prince and Bholu.
   CBI charge sheet: As per analysis of page 15, paragraph 38.
   CBI charge sheet: As per page 13, paragraph 33.
   CBI charge sheet: As per document 205. Bholu's statement recorded on 15 September 2017 by SHO Narender Khatana and filed with the CBI charge sheet.
   As per Bholu's statement recorded at the Gurugram court on the request of the Gurugram Police on 19 September 2017, which is filed with the CBI charge sheet as document 205.

Notes

    The same is mentioned on page 40 of the list of documents in the CBI charge sheet.
    As per the CBI sources.
3. CBI charge sheet: As per page 13, paragraph 33.
    CBI charge sheet: As per document 205. Bholu's statement was recorded by SHO Narender Khatana on 15 September 2017. The same is mentioned on page 40 of the list of documents in the CBI charge sheet.
    As per Bholu's statement recorded at the Gurugram court on the request of the Gurugram Police on 19 September 2017, which is filed with the CBI charge sheet as document 205.
    The same is mentioned on page 40 of the list of documents in the CBI charge sheet.
4. CBI charge sheet: As per page 12, paragraph 28.
    CBI charge sheet: As per Jairaj's statement recorded by the CBI on 30 November 2017 at the CBI office, New Delhi, and filed with the CBI charge sheet.
5. CBI charge sheet: As per pages 10 and 11, paragraph 25.
    CBI charge sheet: As per Harjot's statement recorded by the CBI at the CBI office, New Delhi, on 27 December 2017 and filed with the CBI charge sheet.
6. CBI charge sheet: As per pages 13 and 14, paragraph 35.
    CBI charge sheet: As per Tarun's statement recorded by the CBI at the BSF Campus, Sohna Road, Gurugram, on 28 October 2017 and filed with the CBI charge sheet.
    CBI charge sheet: As per document D197. Tarun's statement recorded under section 164 of the CrPC at the Saket court, New Delhi, on the request of the CBI on 8 January 2018.
7. CBI charge sheet: As per page 14, paragraph 36.

Notes

8. CBI charge sheet: As per page 15, paragraph 39.
9. CBI charge sheet: As per page 20, paragraph 49.
   CBI charge sheet: As per Dr Deepak Mathur's statement recorded by the CBI on 19 January 2018 at the CBI office, New Delhi, and filed with the CBI charge sheet.
10. CBI charge sheet: As per page 16, paragraph 41.
    CBI charge sheet: As per Ankita's statement recorded by the CBI on 20 October 2017 at Gurugram and filed with the CBI charge sheet.
    CBI charge sheet: As per page 17, paragraph 43.
    CBI charge sheet: As per document D190. Ankita's statement recorded under section 164 of the CrPC on 16 January 2018 at the Saket court, New Delhi, on the request of the CBI and filed with the CBI charge sheet.
11. CBI charge sheet: As per pages 16 and 17, paragraph 42.
    CBI charge sheet: As per Ayushman's statement recorded by the CBI on 20 October 2017 at Gurugram and filed with the CBI charge sheet.
    CBI charge sheet: As per page 17, paragraph 43.
    CBI charge sheet: As per document D191. Ayushman's statement recorded under section 164 of the CrPC on 16 January 2018 at the Saket court, New Delhi, on the request of the CBI and filed with the CBI charge sheet.
12. CBI charge sheet: As per page 24, paragraph 60.
    CBI charge sheet: As per document D80 and D82.
13. CBI charge sheet: As per page 24, paragraph 60.
    CBI charge sheet: As per document D68.
14. CBI charge sheet: As per pages 14 and 15, paragraph 37.
    CBI charge sheet: As per page 21, paragraph 51.
    CBI charge sheet: As per document D86 regarding the search at Bholu's residence and seizure of articles.

CBI charge sheet: As per pages 22 to 24, paragraphs 55, 56, 57 and 58.

CBI charge sheet: As per document 110 (181 pages). CBI charge sheet: As per the statements of the independent witnesses recorded by the CBI on 10 November 2017 at the CBI office, New Delhi, and filed with the CBI charge sheet.

9. The Confession

1. CBI charge sheet: As per page 20, paragraph 50.
   CBI charge sheet: As per document 102.
   CBI charge sheet: As per statements of two independent witnesses recorded by the CBI on 8 November 2017 at the CBI office, New Delhi, and filed with the CBI charge sheet.
   CBI charge sheet: As per the statement of the CBI welfare officer, R.K. Dutta, recorded by the CBI on 8 November 2017 at the CBI office, New Delhi, and filed with the CBI charge sheet.
   CBI charge sheet: As per the statement of the sub-inspector and junior welfare police officer of the Lodhi Colony police station, Prakash Chand, recorded by the CBI on 8 November 2017 at the CBI office, New Delhi, and filed with the CBI charge sheet.
2. CBI charge sheet: As per page 21, paragraph 51.
   CBI charge sheet: As per the statement of the sub-inspector and junior welfare police officer of the Lodhi Colony police station, Prakash Chand, recorded by the CBI on 8 November 2017 at the CBI office, New Delhi, and filed with the CBI charge sheet.

Notes

CBI charge sheet: As per document D104.

CBI charge sheet: As per document D110.

CBI charge sheet: As per independent witness statements recorded by the CBI on 10 November 2017 at the CBI office, New Delhi, and filed with the CBI charge sheet.

CBI charge sheet: As per statements of two independent witnesses recorded by the CBI on 8 November 2017 at the CBI office, New Delhi, and filed with the CBI charge sheet.

CBI charge sheet: As per the statement of the CBI welfare officer, R.K. Dutta, recorded by the CBI on 8 November 2017 at the CBI office, New Delhi, and filed with the CBI charge sheet.

CBI charge sheet: As per the statement of the sub-inspector and junior welfare police officer of the Lodhi Colony police station, Prakash Chand, recorded by the CBI on 8 November 2017 at the CBI office, New Delhi, and filed with the CBI charge sheet.

3. Interview with Nisha Saini and Principal Magistrate Devender Singh on 25 November 2017.
4. CBI charge sheet: As per pages 22 and 23, paragraph 52. CBI charge sheet: As per document D106 regarding the order passed by the principal magistrate, JJB, Gurugram, for police custody of the child in conflict with law, Bholu.
5. Interview with Ajay Kumar Bassi.
6. CBI charge sheet: As per page 22, paragraphs 53 and 54. CBI charge sheet: As per the independent witness's statement recorded by the CBI on 9 November 2017 at the CBI office, New Delhi, and filed with the CBI charge sheet.

CBI charge sheet: As per the independent witness's statement recorded by the CBI on 25 January 2018 at Gurugram and filed with the CBI charge sheet.

CBI charge sheet: As per documents 107 and 108.
7. CBI charge sheet: As per documents 107 and 108.
8. Interview with Dr Joginder Singh Kairo on 6 December 2017.
9. Interviews with Nisha Saini and Ajay Kumar Bassi in November 2017.

10. The Reports

1. Interviews with Nisha Saini and Ajay Kumar Bassi in November 2017.
2. Ibid.
3. Ibid.
4. Interview with Nisha Saini.
5. CBI charge sheet: As per statement recorded by the CBI on 10 November 2017 at the CBI office, New Delhi, and filed with the CBI charge sheet.
6. As per the JJB, Gurugram. Order dated 20 December 2017.
7. Ibid.
   CBI charge sheet: As per statement recorded by the CBI on 23 December 2017 at the CBI office, New Delhi, and filed with the CBI charge sheet.
8. As per the JJB, Gurugram. Order dated 20 December 2017.
   CBI charge sheet: As per Manika Govind's statement recorded by the CBI on 17 November 2017 at the CBI office, New Delhi, and filed with the CBI charge sheet.
   CBI charge sheet: As per document D202. Manika Govind's statement recorded under section 164 of the CrPC at the Saket court, New Delhi, and filed with the CBI charge sheet.
9. As per the JJB, Gurugram. Order dated 20 December 2017.
10. Ibid.

Notes

This was what Bholu's neighbours had to say. This is also as per the social investigation report filed by Nisha Saini.
11. As per the JJB, Gurugram. Order dated 20 December 2017.
12. CBI charge sheet: As per pages 24 and 25, paragraph 61. As per the JJB, Gurugram. Order dated 20 December 2017.
13. As per the JJB, Gurugram. Order dated 20 December 2017.
14. Meetings with Dr Joginder Singh Kairo in December 2017 at PGIMS Rohtak.
15. CBI charge sheet: As per page 27, paragraph 71.
    CBI charge sheet: As per Nitin's statement recorded by the CBI on 7 November 2017 at the CBI office, New Delhi, and filed with the CBI charge sheet.
    CBI charge sheet: As per document D198. Nitin's statement recorded under section 164 of the CrPC at the Saket court, New Delhi, on 5 January 2018 and filed with the CBI charge sheet.
16. CBI charge sheet: As per page 17, paragraph 44.
    CBI charge sheet: As per Ayushman's statement recorded by the CBI on 31 October 2017 at the BSF Campus, Sohna Road, Gurugram, and filed with the CBI charge sheet.
    CBI charge sheet: As per document D195. Ayushman's statement recorded under section 164 of the CrPC at the Saket court, New Delhi, on 8 January 2018 and filed with the CBI charge sheet.
17. CBI charge sheet: As per pages 18 to 20, paragraphs 45 to 48.
    CBI charge sheet: As per statement recorded by the CBI on 1 November 2017 at the BSF Campus, Gurugram, and filed with the CBI charge sheet.
    CBI charge sheet: As per document D194. Statement recorded under section 164 of the CrPC at the Saket court,

New Delhi, on 5 January 2018 and filed with the CBI charge sheet.

CBI charge sheet: As per statement recorded by the CBI on 1 November 2017 at the BSF Campus, Gurugram, and filed with the CBI charge sheet. CBI charge sheet: As per document D193. Statement recorded under section 164 of the CrPC at the Saket court, New Delhi, on 5 January 2018 and filed with the CBI charge sheet.

CBI charge sheet: As per statement recorded by the CBI on 26 December 2017 at the CBI office, New Delhi, and filed with the CBI charge sheet.

CBI charge sheet: As per document D192. Statement recorded under section 164 of the CrPC at the Saket court, New Delhi, on 5 January 2018 and filed with the CBI charge sheet.

CBI charge sheet: As per statement recorded by the CBI on 13 December 2017 at the CBI office, New Delhi, and filed with the CBI charge sheet.

CBI charge sheet: As per document D201. Statement recorded under section 164 of the CrPC at the Saket court, New Delhi, on 5 January 2018 and filed with the CBI charge sheet.

CBI charge sheet: As per statement recorded by the CBI on 15 January 2018 at the CBI office, New Delhi, and filed with the CBI charge sheet.

CBI charge sheet: As per document D199. Statement recorded under section 164 of the CrPC at the Saket court, New Delhi, on 5 January 2018 and filed with the CBI charge sheet.

CBI charge sheet: As per statement recorded by the CBI on

Notes

    1 December 2017 at the CBI office, New Delhi, and filed with the CBI charge sheet.
CBI charge sheet: As per document D200. Statement recorded under section 164 of the CrPC at the Saket court, New Delhi, on 5 January 2018 and filed with the CBI charge sheet.

18. CBI charge sheet: As per page 26, paragraph 66.
CBI charge sheet: As per statement recorded by the CBI on 23 December 2017 at the CBI office, New Delhi, and filed with the CBI charge sheet.
19. CBI charge sheet: As per pages 19 and 20, paragraph 48.
CBI charge sheet: As per statement recorded by the CBI on 1 December 2017 at the CBI office, New Delhi, and filed with the CBI charge sheet.
20. CBI charge sheet: As per page 26, paragraph 68.
CBI charge sheet: As per statement recorded by the CBI on 23 December 2017 at the CBI office, New Delhi, and filed with the CBI charge sheet.

11. A Family in Despair

1. Interview with Bholu's mother on 5 November 2018.
2. Ibid.
3. Ibid.
4. This fact is explained in the statements of employees of the company that had installed CCTV cameras in the school, recorded by the CBI on 8 January 2018 at the CBI office, New Delhi, and filed with the CBI charge sheet.
5. Interview with Bholu's father on 5 November 2018.
6. Several interviews with Bholu's parents on 12, 15, 19 and 20 December 2017, 15 January 2018 and 21 May 2018.
7. Ibid.

12. 'Tareekh pe Tareekh'

1. https://www.hindustantimes.com/cities/gurugram-news/ggm-murder-accused-to-be-tried-as-an-adult-101666029509311.html
2. https://timesofindia.indiatimes.com/city/gurgaon/2017-school-murder-sc-dismisses-accuseds-plea-against-trial-as-adult/articleshow/105025442.cms
3. https://timesofindia.indiatimes.com/city/gurgaon/2017-school-murder-sc-dismisses-accuseds-plea-against-trial-as-adult/articleshow/105025442.cms
4. As per Additional Sessions Judge J.S. Kundu, Gurugram. Order dated 5 February 2018.
5. As per the Punjab and Haryana High Court order/judgment dated 6 June 2018 passed by Honourable Mrs Justice Daya Chaudhary.
6. https://www.hindustantimes.com/cities/gurugram-news/gurugram-school-murder-sc-grants-bail-to-accused-after-five-years-in-detention-101666261766985.html
7. As per the JJB order dated 3 April 2018. The author possesses a copy of the order.
8. Interview with Dinesh Yadav, superintendent of the Faridabad observation centre, on 19 April 2019.
9. As per the JJB order dated 3 April 2018.

13. Road to the Trial

1. https://www.hindustantimes.com/cities/gurugram-news/charges-framed-against-man-accused-in-gurugram-private-school-murder-101674662093787.html
2. https://www.hindustantimes.com/cities/gurugram-news/

after-more-than-five-years-trial-begins-in-ggm-school-murder-case-101676918537610.html
3. https://timesofindia.indiatimes.com/city/gurgaon/gurgaon-school-murder-seller-of-knife-fails-to-identify-accused/articleshow/101999613.cms
4. https://timesofindia.indiatimes.com/city/gurgaon/trial-too-slow-court-asks-cbi-to-seek-more-dates/articleshow/102847341.cms

14. Three Families

1. Several interviews with Bhaskar Thakkar on 8 and 15 September 2017, 12 October 2017, 15 November 2017, 21 November 2017, 2 January 2018 and 11 February 2018.
2. Several interviews with Bhaskar Thakkar on 8 and 15 September 2017, 12 October 2017, 15 November 2017, 21 November 2017, 2 January 2018 and 11 February 2018.
3. Several interviews with Bholu's father on 12, 15, 19 and 20 December 2017, 15 January 2018 and 21 May 2018.
4. https://www.hindustantimes.com/gurgaon/bhondsi-school-murder-conductor-refuses-rs1l-compensation/story-oRXJGPmXqiqhPjLDu2xMOP.html
5. https://www.hindustantimes.com/gurugram/cbi-files-chargesheet-against-four-police-officials-in-school-murder-case/story-etwD9pwNRm9mNZngsD3ZnO.html
6. https://www.hindustantimes.com/cities/gurugram-news/gurugram-school-murder-cbi-court-raps-govt-police-over-delay-in-prosecuting-four-cops-101612289026157.html

15. The School

1. Interview with Kajal on 15 October 2017.
2. Interview with Sudha Goyal on 15 October 2017.
3. Interview with Principal Erry on 15 October 2017.
4. Interview with Neeti Kaushik on 15 October 2017.
5. Interview with Saloni on 15 October 2017.
6. Interview with Tripti Singh Rathore on 15 October 2017.
7. Interview with Neela Kaushik on 15 October 2017.
8. Several interviews with Ajay Kumar Bassi on 20 December 2017, 15 January 2018 and 21 May 2018.
9. Ibid.
10. Ibid.
11. Interviews with Nisha Saini in November 2017.
12. Interviews with Bholu's mother.
13. Interview with Tarun in November 2017. Interview with some of Bholu's classmates in November 2017. They refused to quote their names.

    Interview with Nisha Saini in November 2017.

    CBI charge sheet: As per page 27, paragraph 71.

    CBI charge sheet: As per pages 17 and 18, paragraph 44 – Ayushman's statement.

    CBI charge sheet: As per pages 17 and 18, paragraph 45. Statements were recorded at the CBI headquarters and the Saket court, New Delhi.

    CBI charge sheet: As per page 18, paragraph 46.

Acknowledgements

Completing this book was a challenge that I could not have conquered without the guidance of my bureau chief, Neha Pushkarna, who toiled over my language and grammar, and expanded my knowledge of storytelling. She has been a constant source of strength and has always gone the extra mile to make my work and narration compelling. Thank you for making every line count.

Author's Note

There was nothing unusual about that Friday morning at the *Hindustan Times* office till I received a call from one of my sources about a student who had been murdered at a school in Gurugram. I hadn't been covering crime for a year; I was covering other topics such as wildlife, civic beats, lifestyle, forest, education and the like. When I called up my boss to inform him, his first instruction was, 'Then rush to the spot immediately!' I hesitated at first as it was not my area to cover, but his mandate was simple and definite, and so I dashed from the Gurugram office to the school.

When I reached the location, I was among the first people that had gathered outside the school premises. I made my way inside and saw the toilet which was the scene of the crime. It was freshly splattered with

Author's Note

blood all over, and I even saw the knife lying in the commode. The sight was dreadful, and I knew I had to get into action mode right away. I started gathering as much information as I could from the teachers and staff standing around the toilet. A short while later, a lot of parents began gathering and the media started arriving as well. But since I was there before anyone, I could get first-hand information by interviewing people who were present in the school at the exact moment the incident had taken place, which was essentially a challenge for others in the media.

When I learnt about Amit Kumar, the conductor of one of the school buses, and his rather quick arrest by the police, I went to his village Ghamroj and met his wife, Mala. I was not convinced since day one that Amit had murdered the victim. I knew that something was fishy and that's what drove me to continuously look for more, and I was the sole reporter to file exclusive stories for this case. My report published in the *Hindustan Times* broke the news that Mala and the other villagers in his neighbourhood had pooled their money to hire a lawyer from Rohtak to fight Amit's case.

It was not easy to build a network of sources because people were extremely hesitant to talk about

Author's Note

the horrific murder of a child inside a school, and understandably so. For instance, Harjot, the school gardener, refused to talk to me. But I never lost hope along the way. I had built an extensive network in the school by virtue of being the first one to arrive. I was being informed of every little development such as when the CBI was scheduled to arrive, when the police were patrolling the area, etc. I spoke to the staff at the school: the school coordinator who had asked Amit to carry the victim's body to the hospital; the physical education teacher who had seen the knife in the commode; the school principal who was suspended; Jairaj, who drove Amit and the victim to the hospital; the teacher in Bholu's class. I spoke to a number of students who had been Bholu's classmates for a while. There was a small plot outside the Gurugram school building where vegetable vendors would sit with their carts. I have spent hours sitting and eating with them and working towards building a good rapport with them so that they could help me with information.

I was in constant contact with Prince's parents, Jaya and Bhaskar Thakkar. Despite the immeasurable loss of their son, they used to call me two to three times a day and give me any and every information they had.

Author's Note

I conducted several interviews with the IOs of the CBI, Ajay Kumar Bassi and Narender Khatana, who gave me exclusive access to the statements recorded by witnesses and suspects, as well as the CBI charge sheet. I interviewed DCP Deepak Saharan, DCP Sumit Kuhar and DCP Amit Bakshi. The Gurugram Police were very cooperative and helped me with all the information I needed to file my reports. I had several conversations with Amit and interviewed his lawyer Mohit Verma who was instrumental in his release. I was the only reporter who managed to get access and meet Bholu. I was present for all his hearings in the court and spoke at length with his parents. I had made trustworthy contacts at the Child Welfare Committee as well as the JJB, which helped me with information about Bholu. I conducted several interviews with Nisha Saini, the legal-cum-probation officer from the District Child Protection Unit, whose social investigation report was immensely helpful.

For a complete list of interviewees, sources and documents referred to, please refer to the endnotes for each chapter.

All in all, I interviewed and spoke to every person a reporter could to write and file the most authentic stories that did justice to the case. I am lucky that I

Author's Note

got this opportunity. My sources provided exclusive details that helped me fill the gaps in my narrative. Thus, I had all this information which other reporters never had access to. People used to rely on the *Hindustan Times* reports for speed and authenticity of facts on this case.

When the incident happened, my son had just taken his class twelve exams and was still a teenager. I could sympathize with Jaya Thakkar and I connected with the family at an emotional level, which played a huge role in my reporting of this case. For a reporter, travelling from one location to another and filing stories is very taxing. The *Hindustan Times* wanted exclusive stories every day and our bosses compared newspapers to check the quality of stories filed and if we had missed out on anything. So the pressure was immense and, at times, it was very challenging. But with all the support, trust, presence of mind and hard work, I was able to get the information I needed.

A Note on the Author

Leena Dhankhar has been a journalist at the *Hindustan Times* for fifteen years and specializes in reporting on crime, special investigations and juvenile justice. As chief correspondent, she has emerged as one of the city's foremost crime journalists – with an unparalleled knowledge of Gurugram's gang wars and history. This is her first book.